THE ART
OF AUDUBON

THE ART OF AUDUBON

The Complete Birds and Mammals

JOHN JAMES AUDUBON

With an Introduction by Roger Tory Peterson

Times
BOOKS

Published by TIMES BOOKS, a division
of Quadrangle/The New York Times Book Co., Inc.
Three Park Avenue, New York, N.Y. 10016

Published simultaneously in Canada by
Fitzhenry & Whiteside, Ltd., Toronto.

Library of Congress Cataloging in Publication Data

Audubon, John James, 1785–1851.
    The art of Audubon.

    Includes index.
    1. Birds—North America—Pictorial works.
2. Mammals—North America—Pictorial works.
I. Title.
QL681.A96 1979   599'.09'70222   79-51434
ISBN 0-8129-0841-4

Manufactured in the United States of America.

Contents

BIRDS BY FAMILY

MAMMALS BY GENUS

Introduction

Although John James Audubon was an emigre from France when he came to the United States at the age of eighteen, he was actually born in the West Indies in the year 1785. His mother was a genteel French-Creole lady and his father a prosperous French sea-captain, who after reverses in Les Cayes in Santo Domingo, now Haiti, where he owned an estate, returned to France. There the youthful Jean Jacques Fougere Audubon received a young gentleman's tutoring and even studied drawing under the guidance of the master, Jacques Louis David.

Audubon's odyssey in North America has been recounted many times; how his father sent him to his farm at Mill Grove near Philadelphia, and later set him up in business in Kentucky where he met with successive business failures as he moved westward to the Mississippi and then down to New Orleans. There his devoted wife, Lucy, supported herself and their two sons while her wandering husband was away many months at a time exploring the wilderness, painting, and prodigiously pursuing his dream of producing the epic work on the birds of North America.

Elemental forces were at work within Audubon—the stuff of which artists, poets and prophets are made. Birds were the hub around which his world revolved; their furious pace of living, their beauty, their mystery, reflected the subtle forces that guided his own life.

He was unworldly, yet closely attuned to the natural world. His simplicity, tremendous vitality, enthusiasm for life in all its variety, and his drive for creative excellence made him one of the most enduring personalities in American history.

Audubon's portraits of birds, the product of more than thirty years of field work and labor at the drawing board, were engraved by Robert Havell, Jr. of London who undertook the herculean eleven-year task of reproduction and even introduced minor changes of his own into some of the compositions and backgrounds. They were published as "The Birds of America" in four huge volumes (the largest weighing 56 pounds) between the years of 1827 and 1838. In his 435 color plates, Audubon depicted the birds exactly the size of life. Even the oversize format, known as "double elephant folio," the largest ever attempted in the history of book publishing, was insufficient to accommodate the large birds comfortably, with the result that tall birds such as the flamingo and the great blue heron are shown with their long necks drooped toward their feet. On the other hand, tiny birds like kinglets and hummingbirds are all but lost on the page.

Although Audubon's immortality rests largely on his work as an artist, he was no less of an ornithologist. The extraordinary amount of observation detailed in his five-volume, three thousand-page *Ornithological Biography*, edited and rewritten in part by William Mac-Gillivray and published almost concurrently with his *Birds of America* between the years of 1831 and 1839 as a supplemental descriptive text relating to the plates, remains as the baseline for comparing the status of birds then and now. No less important as an historical record are the comments they contain on places, people and customs.

Later, Audubon prepared a seven-volume octavo edition of his *Birds of America*, adding 65 more color plates and incorporating the text from his *Ornithological Biography*. This first octavo edition was published in New York and Philadelphia between the years of 1840 and 1844.

In reviewing Audubon's massive tour-de-force, his paintings seem to fall into at least three categories. We usually think of Audubon's style as patternistic or decorative on an open white background. Actually, the leaves, flowers and other accessories were often painted in by apprentice artists, notably Joseph Mason and George Lehman. At a later period he produced many bird portraits with solid environmental backgrounds, usually southern scenes, which were executed largely by Lehman. Among the last few plates and the 65 additional ones included in the later octavo edition are birds from the western part of the country. These are perhaps his least successful efforts. He may have grown tired of his seemingly endless projects, but a fairer judgment is that he had seen few of these birds in life. They are drawn from specimens sent to him by Nuttall, Swainson, Townsend, and Gould.

It was inevitable that after he had painted and described all the birds then known from North America, Audubon would apply his brush and pen to the mammals with which he also had a lifelong intimacy.

In the Harvard University Library there is a crayon sketch of a marmot dashed off by Audubon when he revisited France at the age of twenty. It is believed to be his earliest drawing of a mammal. Even when he was deeply involved with his bird portraiture he occasionally found time to draw mammals. A recurrent theme was an otter in a trap, which he painted again and again both in watercolor and in oils, particularly when he was in need of funds. A particularly skilled version was hung in an exhibition at the Scottish Academy.

Actually, Audubon conceived the idea of a comparable mammal publication several years earlier during conversations with the Reverend John Bachman of South Carolina, himself a naturalist of considerable scholarship, who warned Audubon of the technical problems they faced. He emphasized that mammals, because of their more secretive habits, would be more difficult to paint and to write about than birds. It was agreed that Bachman would act as co-author and editor of the three biographical volumes which were to accompany the three-volume folio of mammal portraits. The whole enterprise was impressively titled *The Viviparous Quadrupeds of North America.*

Audubon's two grown sons, John and Victor, had become full-fledged assistants in the production of his *Birds of America* by 1836. Both were learning to paint creditably, and John Woodhouse Audubon in particular gave promise of a talent that could equal his father's. The two boys married the two elder daughters of the Reverend Bachman, a family merger that was to end tragically when John's wife Maria, then 23, died of tuberculosis, leaving two small children. She was followed in death less than a year later by Victor's wife, Mary Eliza, plunging Audubon into the greatest grief he had known since the death of his own two infant daughters.

Bachman felt it was very important that Audubon, then in his late fifties, should go west to investigate some of the mammals of the frontier. His trip in 1843 to the headwaters of the Missouri and the mouth of the Yellowstone was his last great field expedition. After risking death at the hands of Sioux and Assiniboines and other adventures, he returned to his New York City estate, Minniesland, where he devoted his waning energies to the *Quadrupeds* which were to be published by J. T. Bowen of Philadelphia. His eyes and his mind were no longer equal to the strain, so in 1846 he began to rely more on his two talented sons. He had already painted more than 100 of the 150 colorplates. His son John painted the rest under close supervision while Victor skillfully put in the backgrounds. The remainder of the biographies were entirely the work of Reverend Bachman.

Audubon did not live to see the *Quadrupeds* completed. He died in 1851 at the age of 66.

Audubon might rightly have been called the "Father of American Ornithology" had not the Scot, Alexander Wilson, preceded him by about twenty years in the publication of his own *American Ornithology.* Although Wilson was able to find a publisher in the United States, Audubon had to go to England to find backers and printers for his larger, more ambitious folio of paintings. A total of about 190 sets were eventually bound and distributed. Less than half exist today; the others were acquired by dealers who broke them up and sold the prints individually.

Twelve years after Audubon's death, his widow sold his original paintings to the New York Historical Society where they can be seen to this day, forever safeguarded.

Audubon was the epitome of the hunter-naturalist. Modern critics sometimes point out that as a young man he found too much delight in shooting birds; he was "in blood up to his elbows." This is abundantly borne out by his *Ornithological Biography* in which he details the number of specimens he took, often far more than he needed for his portraits or his anatomical studies.

It would therefore seem inappropriate that the foremost conservation organization in the United States should adopt his name, but not so. Actually, Audubon was ahead of his time. Like so many thoughtful sportsmen since, he eventually developed a conservation conscience. In an era when there were no game laws, no national parks or refuges, when vulnerable nature gave way to human pressures and often sheer stupidity, when there was no environmental ethic, he was a witness who sounded the alarm. He became more and more concerned during his later travels when, with the perspective of his years, he could see the trend. He wrote vividly and passionately about what he saw and some of the passages in his writings were very prophetic.

Today Audubon, who wished to be known primarily as an artist, is considered the patron saint of American wildlife conservation. His name, long synonymous with birds, has become a symbol of our need to understand the environment and to live in harmony with all that is natural.

And as long as our civilization lasts, America will be in debt to this genius.

Roger Tory Peterson

PUBLISHER'S NOTE

One of the last major publishing projects on which John James Audubon embarked was the complete Octavo edition of his paintings. Containing 500 engravings of birds, partially revised from the original "double elephant folio" edition, the Octavo edition was finally published in seven volumes in the 1840s. Until now, the Octavo edition of Audubon's birds together with his 150 engravings of *Quadrupeds* have never been assembled and published in a single volume.

The bird and mammal sections have been separately arranged in a logical pattern to provide clear comparison within each individual species. Following a scientific order originally devised by Audubon, the publisher has divided the bird engravings by family and sub-divided them by genus. With each individual genus, the birds have been alphabetically positioned according to the first name on the engraving. The mammals have been grouped by Latin genus name, and the genus names have subsequently been alphabetized.

Over the years many changes have been made in Audubon's scientific names. For example, *Bison Americanus* is now *Bison Bison; Ursa Ferox* is now *Ursa Horribilis.* Also, Audubon divided the cats into two classifications *(Felis* and *Lynx),* a distinction that is no longer in use. There are undoubtedly many other changes which have come about in scientific nomenclature since the 1840s, but this new edition is as close to Audubon's original designations as is possible.

At the end of the volume, two indices have been provided, separately listing the birds and mammals within an English-Latin and Latin-English context.

BOOK OF BIRDS

Pl. 3

Drawn from Nature by J.J. Audubon, F.R.S.F.L.S.

Black Vulture or Carrion Crow.

Lith. printed & Col.d by J.T. Bowen, Phil.a

Pl. 1

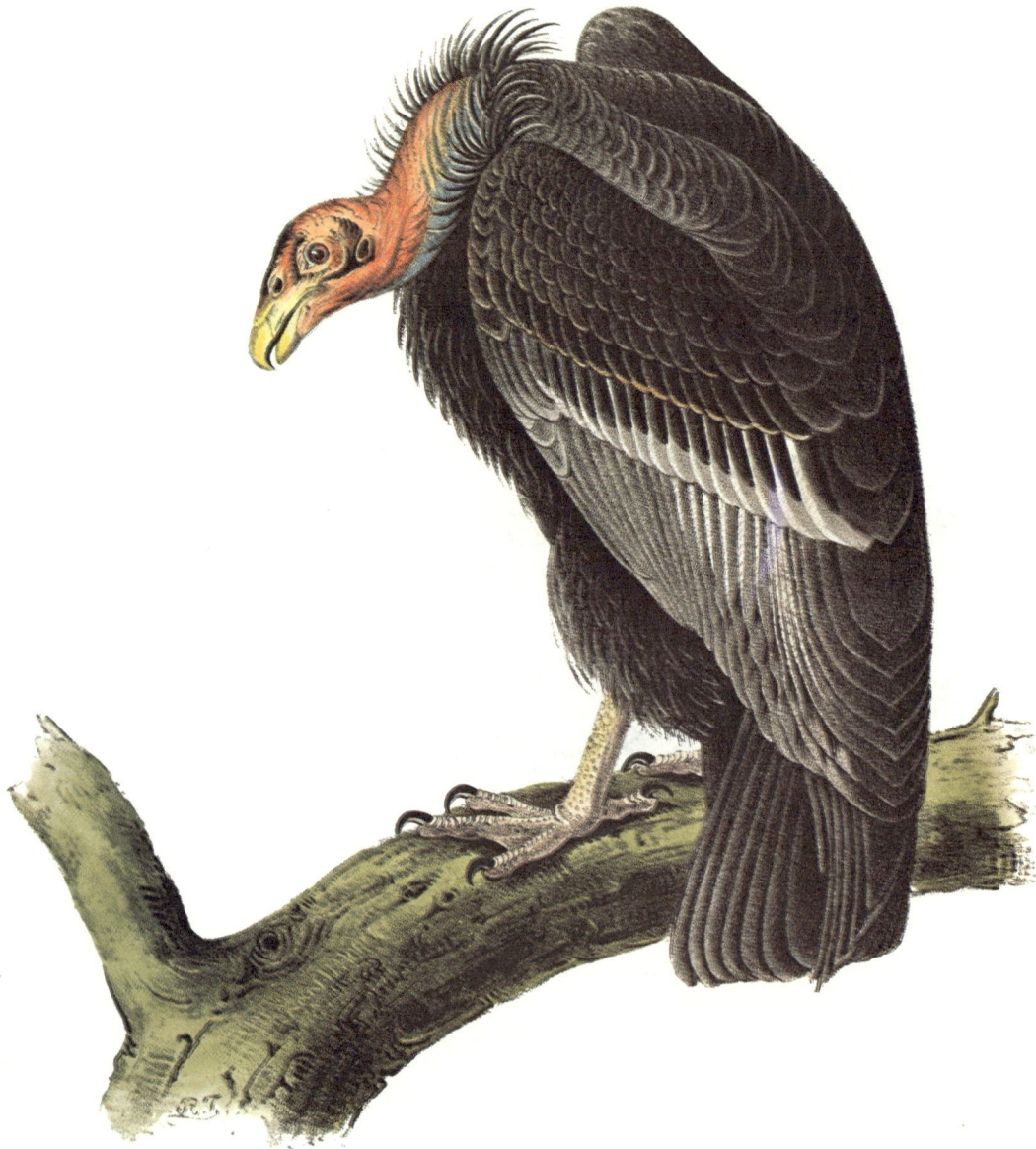

Californian Turkey Vulture

Drawn from Nature by J.J. Audubon, F.R.S.F.L.S.   Lith.ᵈ, printed & Col.ᵈ by J. T. Bowen, Phil.ᵃ

Pl. 2

Red.-headed Turkey Vulture.

Drawn from Nature by J.J.Audubon, F.R.S.F.L.S.   Lith. printed & Col.d by J. T. Bowen, Phil.a

Caracara   Eagle

Drawn from Nature by J.J. Audubon F.R.S.F.L.S.   Lith. printed & Col.d by J.T. Bowen, Phil.a

Pl. 10.

Broad-winged Buzzard.

Drawn from Nature by J.J.Audubon.F.R.S.F.L..

Lith? Printed & Col? by J.T.Bowen.Philad?

Pl. 6

Common Buzzard.

COMMON BUZZARD.

Drawn from Nature by J.J.Audubon, F.R.S.F.L.S.

Harlan's Buzzard.

Drawn from Nature by J.J.Audubon,F.R.S.F.L.S.   Lithd Printed & Cold by J. T. Bowen, Philada

Harris's Buzzard

Drawn from Nature by J. J. Audubon, F.R.S.F.L.S.

Lith. printed & Col.d by J. T. Bowen, Phil.a

Red-shouldered Buzzard

Drawn from Nature by J.J.Audubon,F.R.S.F.L.S.   Lith.ª Printed & Col.ᵈ by J. T. Bowen, Philad.ª

Red-tailed Buzzard.

Drawn from Nature by J.J.Audubon,F.R.S.F.L.S.   Lith.d Printed & Col.d by J.T.Bowen, Philad.a

Pl. II.

R.T.
Rough-legged Buzzard.

Drawn from nature by J.J.Audubon F.R.S.F.L.S.

Lith.d Printed & Col.d by J.T.Bowen.Philad.ª

Pl. 12.

Golden Eagle.

Drawn from Nature by J.J.Audubon. F.R.S.F.L.S.

Lith^d Printed & Col^d by J T Bowen, Philad^a

Pl. 10.

Washington Sea Eagle.

Drawn from Nature by J.J.Audubon F.R.S. F.L.S

Lith.d Printed & Col.d by J.T Bowen Phila.da

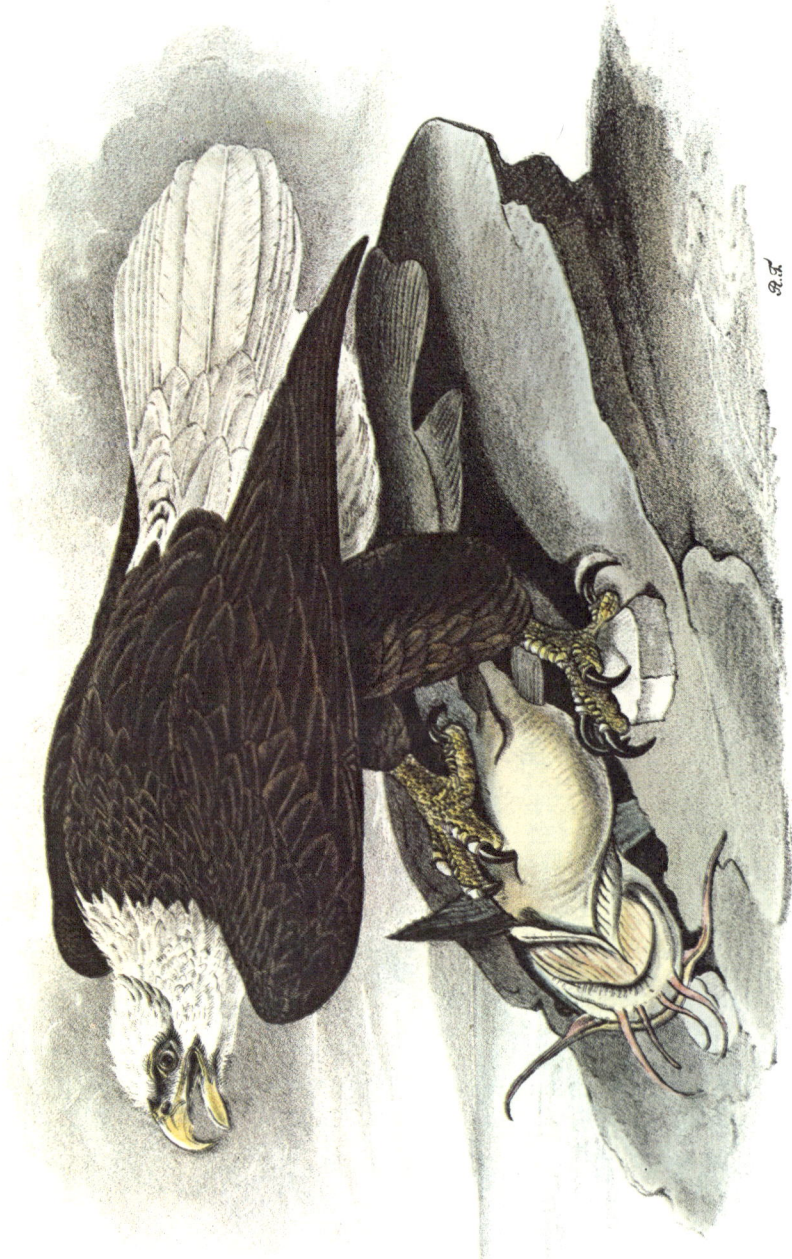

White-headed Sea Eagle, or Bald Eagle.

Drawn from Nature by J.J.Audubon. F.R.S.F.L.S.

Lith.d Printed & Col.d by J.T.Bowen Phila.a

Common Osprey. Fish Hawk!

Drawn from Nature by J.J.Audubon. F.R.S.F.L.S.   Lithᵈ Printed & Colᵈ by J.T.Bowen. Philadᵃ.

Black-shouldered Elanus.

Drawn from Nature by J.J.Audubon. F.R.S.FL.S.   Lithd Printed & Cold by J.T.Bowen. Philada

Mississipi Kite.

Drawn from Nature by J.J.Audubon.F.R.S.F.L.S.   Lithd Printed & Cold by J.T.Bowen.Philada

No. 4

Swallow-tailed Hawk.

20

Iceland or Gyr Falcon.

Drawn from nature by J.J.Audubon.F.R.S.F.L.S.   Lith⁴ Printed & Col⁴ by J.T.Bowen.Philad⁴

Pl. 20

Peregrine Falcon.

Drawn from Nature by J.J.Audubon. F.R.S.F.L.S.

Pigeon Falcon.

Drawn from Nature by J. J. Audubon F.R.S.F.L.S   Lithᵈ Printed & Colᵈ by J T Bowen Philad

Sparrow Falcon.

Drawn from Nature by J.J.Audubon. F.R.S.F.L.S.   Lith⁴. Printed & Col⁴ by J.T.Bowen, Philad⁴.

Goshawk.

Drawn from Nature by J.J.Audubon. F.R.S.F.L.S.   Lith.d Printed & Col.d by J.T. Bowen Philad.a

R.T.

Cooper's Hawk.

Drawn from Nature by J.J. Audubon. F.R.S. F.L.S.   Lith.ᵈ Printed & Col.ᵈ by J.T. Bowen. Philad.ᵃ

Sharp-shinned Hawk.

Drawn from Nature by J.J. Audubon. F.R.S.F.L.S.   Lith.ᵈ Printed & Col.ᵈ by J.T. Bowen. Philad.ᵃ

Pl. 26.

Common Harrier.

Drawn from Nature by J.J. Audubon, F.R.S.F.L.S.

Lith⁴ Printed & Col⁴ by J. T. Bowen, Philad.

Pl. 31.

Burrowing Day-Owl.

Drawn from Nature by J.J.Audubon, F.R.S.F.L.S

Lith⁴ Printed & Col⁴ by J.T. Bowen, Philad⁴

Pl. 30.

Columbian Day-Owl.

Drawn from Nature by J.J.Audubon. F.R.S.F.L.S

Lith⁴ Printed & Col⁴ by J.T.Bowen Philad⁴

Hawk Owl.

Drawn from Nature by J. J. Audubon, F.R.S.F.L.S.

Lithᵈ Printed & Colᵈ by J. T. Bowen, Philadᵃ

Pl 29.

_R.T_

Passerine Day-Owl.

Drawn from Nature by J.J.Audubon.F.R.S.F.L.S.   Lithᵈ Printed & Colᵈ by J.T.Bowen.Philadᵃ

R.T.

Snowy Owl.

Drawn from Nature by J.J.Audubon.F.R.S.F.L.S.   Lithᵈ Printed & Colᵈ by J.T.Bowen.Philadᵃ

Little or Acadian Owl

Common Mouse

Drawn from Nature by J.J.Audubon,F.R.S.F.L.S.   Lith⁴Printed & Col⁴by J. T. Bowen,Philad.ᵃ

Tengmalm's Night-Owl.

Drawn from Nature by J.J.Audubon. F.R.S.F.L.S.   Lithd Printed & Cold by J.T.Bowen.Philada.

Pl. 34

Barn Owl.

Drawn from Nature by J.J.Audubon,F.R.S.F.L.S.

Lithᵈ Printed & Colᵈ by J. T. Bowen, Philadᵃ

Barred Owl.

Drawn from Nature by J.J.Audubon,F.R.S.F.L.S.   Lith?Printed & Col?by J. T. Bowen, Philad?

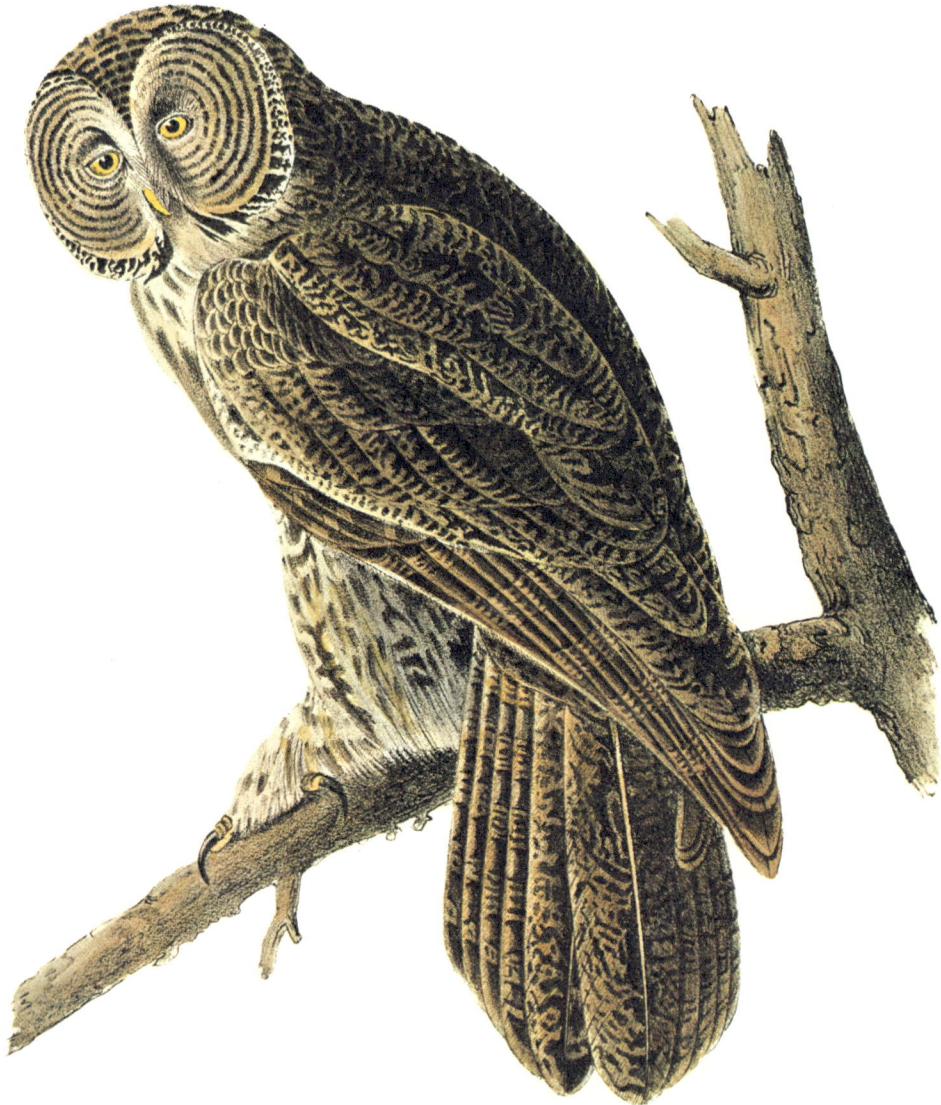

Great Cinereous Owl.

Drawn from Nature by J.J.Audubon,F.R.S.F.L.S.   Lith⁴ Printed & Col⁴ by J. T. Bowen, Philad⁴

Long-eared Owl.

Drawn from Nature by J.J.Audubon.F.R.S.F.L.S.   Lith?. Printed & Col?. by J.T.Bowen.Philad?.

Short-eared Owl.

Drawn from Nature by J.J.Audubon. F.R.S.F.L.S.   Lithd Printed & Cold by J.T. Bowen, Philada

R.T.

Little Screech Owl.
Jersey Pine. Pinus inops.

Drawn from Nature by J. J. Audubon F.R.S.F.L.S.   Lith⁴ Printed & Col⁴ by J.T. Bowen, Philad⁴

Great Horned-Owl.

Drawn from Nature by J.J.Audubon,F.R.S.F.L.S.   Lith⁴ Printed & Col⁴ by J.T.Bowen, Philad⁴

Chuck-will's Widow,
(Harlequin Snake)

Drawn from Nature by J.J.Audubon, F.R.S.F.L.S.   Lithd Printed & Cold by J.T.Bowen, Philada

43

Pl.495.

No.99.

Nuttall's Whip-poor-will
Male

Drawn from Nature by J.J.Audubon F.R.S.F.L.S.

Lith. Printed & Col.d by J.T.Bowen, Philad.a

44

Whip-poor-will

Black Oak or Quercitron. Quercus tinctoria.

Drawn from Nature by J.J.Audubon, F.R.S.F.L.S.   Lith.ᵈ Printed & Col.ᵈ by J. T. Bowen, Philad.ᵃ

Night Hawk.
White Oak. Quercus Alba.

Drawn from Nature by J.J.Audubon.F.R.S.F.L.S.   Lith⁴ Printed & Col⁴ by J.T.Bowen.Philad⁴

American Swift.
(Nests.)

Drawn from Nature by J.J.Audubon. F.R.S.F.L.S.   Lith. Printed & Col. by J.T.Bowen. Philad.

R.T.

Bank Swallow

Drawn from Nature by J.J.Audubon, F.R.S.F.L.S.   Lith.ᵈ Printed & Col.ᵈ by J.T.Bowen, Philad.ᵃ

Barn or Chimney Swallow.

Drawn from Nature by J.J.Audubon F.R.S.F.L

Lithᵈ Printed & Colᵈ by J.T.Bowen,Philadᵃ

R.T.

Cliff Swallow.
(Nests.)

Drawn from Nature by J.J.Audubon, F.R.S.F.L.S.   Lith⁴ Printed & Col⁴ by J.T. Bowen, Philad⁴

Pl. 45.

R.T.

Purple Martin.
(Calabash.)

Drawn from Nature by J.J.Audubon.F.R.S.F.L.S.   Lith⁴ Printed &Col⁴ by J.T.Bowen.Philad⁴

Pl. 51.

Rough-winged Swallow.

Drawn from Nature by J.J.Audubon. F.R.S.F.L.S.

Lith⁴ Printed & Col⁴ by J.T.Bowen, Phila⁴

Violet-Green Swallow.

Drawn from Nature by J.J.Audubon, F.R.S.F.L.

Lith^d Printed & Col^d by J.T.Bowen, Philad^a

Pl. 46.

R.T

White-bellied Swallow.

Drawn from Nature by J.J.Audubon.F.R.S.F.L.S.

Lithᵈ Printed & Colᵈ by J.T.Bowen.Philadᵃ

American Redstart

Virginian Hornbeam or Iron-wood Tree.

1. Male ? Female.

Drawn from Nature by J.J.Audubon, F.R.S.F.L.S.   Lith.ᵈ Printed & Col.ᵈ by J. T. Bowen, Philad.ᵃ.

Pl. 54

Arkansaw Flycatcher.

Drawn from Nature by J.J.Audubon, F.R.S.F.L.S.

Lith⁴ Printed & Col⁴ by J.T. Bowen, Philad⁴

Cooper's Flycatcher.
(*Balsam or Silver Fir. Pinus Balsamea*)
1 Male. 2 Female.

Drawn from Nature by J.J. Audubon, F.R.S.F.L.S.   Lith.d Printed & Col.d by J.T. Bowen. Philad.a

Pl.57.

Great Crested Flycatcher.

Drawn from Nature by J.J. Audubon F.R.S. F.L.S.

Lith.ª Printed & Col.ª by J.T. Bowen Philad.ª

Pl. 491.

R.T.

Least Flycatcher

Male

Drawn from Nature by J.J.Audubon,F.R.S.F.L.S.

Lith. Printed & Col.d by J.T.Bowen, Philad.a

Least Pewee Flycatcher.
White Oak. Quercus Prinus.

Male.

Drawn from Nature by J.J.Audubon.F.R.S.F.L.S

Lith.ᵈ Printed & Col.ᵈ by J.T.Bowen Philad.ᵃ

Pewee Flycatcher.
Cotton Plant. Gossypium. Herbaceum.

1 Male 2 Female

Drawn from Nature by J.J.Audubon.P.R.S.F.L.S.

Lithd. Printed & Cold. by J.T.Bowen.Philad.

Pipiry Flycatcher.
Agati Grandiflora.

Drawn from Nature by J.J.Audubon, F.R.S.F.L.S.   Lithd. Printed & Cold. by J.T.Bowen,Philada.

Pl.60.

Rocky Mountain Flycatcher.
(*Swamp Oak. Quercus Aquatica.*)
Male

Drawn from Nature by J.J.Audubon.F.R.S.F.L.S.

Lith⁴ Printed & Col⁴ by J.T.Bowen.Philad⁴

Say's Flycatcher.

1. Male. 2. Female.

Drawn from Nature by J.J.Audubon. F.R.S.F.L.S.

Lith⁴ Printed & Col⁴ by J.T Bowen, Philad⁴

Pl. 62

Small Green-crested Flycatcher!

Sassafras. Laurus Sassafras.

1 Male. 2 Female.

Drawn from Nature by J.J.Audubon. F.R.S.F.L.S.

Lithd. Printed & Cold. by J.T.Bowen. Philada.

R.T.

Short-legged Pewit Flycatcher.
(Hobble Bush. Viburnum Lantanoides)

Male

Drawn from Nature by J.J. Audubon, F.R.S.F.L.S.   Lithᵈ Printed & Colᵈ by J.T. Bowen, Philadᵃ

Small-headed Flycatcher
Virginian Spider-wort. Tradescantia virginica.
Male

Drawn from Nature by J.J.Audubon. F.R.S.F.L.S.   Lithd Printed & Cold by J.T.Bowen.Phila.

Pl 65.

Traill's Flycatcher
Sweet Gum Liquidambar Styraciflua.

Male

Drawn from Nature by J.J.Audubon F.R.S.F.L.S.

Lith⁴ Printed & Col⁴ by J.T. Bowen Philad⁴

Tyrant Flycatcher or King Bird.
Cotton-wood Populus candicans.

Drawn from Nature by J.J.Audubon. F.R.S.F.L.S.

Lith? Printed & Col? by J.T. Bowen. Philad?

Pl. 64.

Wood Pewee Flycatcher
Swamp Honeysuckle. Azalea Viscosa.

Male

Drawn from Nature by J.J.Audubon, F.R.S.F.L.S.

Lithᵈ Printed & Colᵈ by J.T. Bowen, Philadᵃ

W.E.H.

Yellow-bellied Flycatcher

Male

Drawn from Nature by J.J. Audubon, F.R.S.F.L.S   Lith. Printed & Col.d by J.T.Bowen. Philad.a

Fork-tailed Flycatcher.

Gordonia Lasianthus.

Drawn from Nature by J.J.Audubon.F.R.S.F.L.S.

Lith.d Printed & Col.d by J.T.Bowen.Philad.a

Swallow-tailed Flycatcher.

Drawn from Nature by J.J.Audubon, F.R.S.F.L.S.   Lithᵈ Printed & Colᵈ by J.T.Bowen, Philadᵃ

Pl. 69.

Townsend's Ptilogonys.
Female.

Drawn from Nature by J.J.Audubon.F.R.S.F.L.S.

Lithd Printed & Cold by J.T.Bowen Philad.a

Blue-grey Flycatcher.

Black Walnut. Juglans nigra.

1. Male. 2. Female.

Drawn from Nature by J.J. Audubon, F.R.S.F.L.S.   Lith⁴ Printed & Col⁴ by J.T. Bowen Philad⁴

Bonaparte's Flycatching - Warbler?
Great Magnolia. Magnolia Grandiflora.
Male.

Drawn from Nature by J.J.Audubon. F.R.S.F.L.S.

Lith⁴ Printed & Col⁴ by J.T. Bowen, Philad⁴

Canada Flycatcher.
Great Laurel Rhododendron maximum

1. Male 2. Female.

Drawn from Nature by J.J.Audubon.F.R.S.F.L.S.   Lith Printed & Col^d by J.T.Bowen.Philad^a

Hooded Flycatching Warbler.

Erithryna herbacea.

1. Male. 2. Female.

Drawn from Nature by J.J. Audubon, P.R.S.F.L.S   Lith. Printed & Col.d by J.T. Bowen, Philad.a

Pl. 74

Kentucky Flycatching-Warbler.
Magnolia auriculata.

1 Male. 2 Female.

Drawn from Nature by J.J. Audubon. F.R.S.F.L.S.

Lithᵈ Printed & Colᵈ by J.T. Bowen. Philadᵃ

Wilson's Flycatching-Warbler.
Snakes' Head. Chelone Glabra

1. Male 2. Female.

Drawn from Nature by J.J.Audubon.F.R.S.F.L.S.   Lithᵈ Printed & Colᵈ by J.T.Bowen,Philadᵃ

Audubon's Wood-Warbler.
Strawberry Tree. Euonymus Americanus.
1. Male. 2 Female.

Drawn from Nature by J.J.Audubon, F.R.S.F.L.S.

Lith.ᵈ Printed & Col.ᵈ by J.T. Bowen, Philad.ᵃ

Bay-breasted Wood-Warbler
Highland Cotton-plant. Gossipium herbaceum.

1. Male. 2. Female.

Drawn from Nature by J.J.Audubon. F.R S.F.L.S.   Lithd Printed & Cold by J.T. Bowen, Philada

Black & yellow Wood-Warbler.

1. Male. 2. Female. 3. Young.

Flowering Raspberry. Rubus odoratus.

Drawn from Nature by J.J.Audubon, F.R.S.F.L.S.   Lith⁴ Printed & Col⁴ by J.T. Bowen Philad.ᵃ

Blackburnian Wood-Warbler

1. Male. 2. Female.

Phlox maculata.

Drawn from Nature by J.J.Audubon. F.R.S.F.L.S.   Lithd Printed & Cold by J.T. Bowen. Philada

2.

1.

1.

Black-poll Wood Warbler.
Black Gum Tree. Nyssa aquatica.

1. Males. 2. Female.

Drawn from Nature by J.J.Audubon. F.R.S.F.L.S.

Lith.ᵈ Printed & Col.ᵈ by J.T.Bowen. Philad.ᵃ

Pl. 95.

1.

2.

Black-throated Blue Wood-Warbler.

1 Male 2 Female.
Canadian Columbine.

Drawn from Nature by J.J.Audubon, F.R.S.F.L.S.   Lithd Printed & Cold by J.T. Bowen, Philadª

Black-throated Green Wood Warbler.

Caprifolium Sempervirens

1 Male. 2 Female.

Black-throated Grey Wood-Warbler.

Males.

Drawn from Nature by J.J.Audubon. F.R.S.F.L.S.   Lithᵈ Printed & Colᵈ by J. T. Bowen, Philadᵃ

Blue Mountain Warbler.

Male

Drawn from Nature by J.J.Audubon. F.R.S.F.L.S   Lithd Printed & Cold by J.T Bowen. Philada

Blue yellow-backed Wood-Warbler.

1. Male 2. Female.
Louisiana Flag.

Drawn from Nature by J.J.Audubon, F.R.S.F.L.S.   Lith⁴ Printed & Col⁴ by J.T.Bowen, Philad⁴

Cape May Wood Warbler.

1. Male. 2. Female.

Drawn from Nature by J.J.Audubon, F.R.S.F.L.S.   Lith⁴ Printed & Col⁴ by J.T.Bowen, Philad⁴

Chesnut-sided Wood Warbler.
Moth Mullein. Verbascum Blattaria.

1. Male. 2. Female.

Drawn from Nature by J.J Audubon F.R.S.F.L.S.

Lith⁴ Printed & Col⁴ by J. T. Bowen Phila⁴⁴

Cærulean Wood-Warbler,

1. Old Male. 2. Young Male.

Bear-berry and Spanish Mulberry.

Drawn from Nature by J.J. Audubon, F.R.S. F.L.S.   Lith⁴ Printed & Col⁴ by J.T. Bowen, Philad⁴

Connecticut Warbler.

1. Male. 2. Female.
Gentiana Saponaria.

Drawn from Nature by J.J.Audubon.F.R.S.F.L.S   Lithd Printed & Cold by J.T.Bowen.Philada

Pl. 83.

2.

1.

R. T.

Hemlock Warbler
Dwarf Maple. Acer Spicatum

1. Male 2 Female.

Drawn from Nature by J.J.Audubon. F.R.S.F.L.S.   Lith.ᵈ Printed & Col.ᵈ by J.T.Bowen. Philadᵃ

Hermit Wood-Warbler.

1. Male. 2. Female.

Strawberry Tree.

Drawn from Nature by J.J.Audubon, F.R.S.F.L.S.   Lith⁴ Printed & Col⁴ by J.T.Bowen,Phila⁴⁰

Pine-creeping Wood-Warbler
Yellow Pine. Pinus variabilis.

1. Male 2. Female.

Drawn from Nature by J.J.Audubon, F.R.S.F.L.S.   Lithd Printed & Cold by J.T.Bowen, Philadª

R.T.

Prairie Wood-Warbler.

1. Male. 2. Female.

Buffalo Grass

Drawn from Nature by J.J.Audubon.F.R.S.F.L.S.   Lithᵈ Printed & Colᵈ by J.T.Bowen.Philadᵃ

Rathbone's Wood-Warbler.

1 Male. 2 Female.

Ramping Trumpet-flower.

Drawn from Nature by J.J.Audubon.F.R.S.F.L.S.   Lithᵈ Printed & Colᵈ by J.T.Bowen.Philadᵃ

ℛ.ℱ.

Townsend's Wood-Warbler.

Male.
Carolina Allspice.

Drawn from Nature by J.J.Audubon.P.R.S.F.L.S   Lithᵈ Printed & Colᵈ by J.T Bowen.Philadᵃ

Yellow-crowned Wood-Warbler.

Iris versicolor.

1. Male. 2. Young.

Drawn from Nature by J.J.Audubon, F.R.S.F.L.S.   Lithd Printed & Cold by J.T.Bowen, Philada

Yellow-poll Wood-Warbler.

Males.

Drawn from Nature by J. J. Audubon, F.R.S. F.L.S.　　　　　Lith⁰. Printed & Col⁴ by J.T. Bowen Philad⁴.

Yellow Red-poll Wood-Warbler.
1. *Males.* 2. *Young.*
Wild Orange Tree.

Drawn from Nature by J.J.Audubon, F.R.S.F.L.S.   Lithd Printed & Cold by J.T.Bowen, Philadª

Pl. 79.

Yellow-throated Wood-Warbler.
Chinquapin. Castanea pumila.
Male.

Drawn from Nature by J.J.Audubon.F.R.S.F.L.S.

Lith⁴ Printed & Col⁴ by J.T. Bowen, Philad⁴

Pl. 103.

Drawn from Nature by J.J.Audubon, F.R.S.F.L.S.

Delafield's Ground-Warbler.
Male.

Lith.d Printed & Col.d by J.T.Bowen, Phila.

Macgillivray's Ground-Warbler

1. Male. 2. Female

Drawn from Nature by J.J.Audubon.F.R.S.F.L.S.   Lith.ᵈ Printed & Col.ᵈ by J.T.Bowen.Philad.ᵃ

Maryland Ground-Warbler.

1 Adult Male. 2 Young Male. 3 Female
Bitter wood Tree Viburnum prunifolium.

Drawn from Nature by J.J. Audubon, F.R.S. F.L.S.   Lithd Printed & Cold by J.T. Bowen, Philada

Mourning Ground-Warbler.

Male.

Pheasant's-eye Flos-Adonis.

Drawn from Nature by J.J. Audubon, F.R.S.F.L.S   Lithd. Printed & Cold by J.T Bowen, Philadª

Bachman's Swamp-Warbler.

1. Male. 2. Female

Gordonia pubescens.

Drawn from Nature by J.J.Audubon.F.R.S.F.L.S.   Lith.d Printed & Col.d by J.T.Bowen.Philad.a

Pl. 111.

Blue-winged Yellow Swamp Warbler.

1. Male 2. Female

Cotton Rose. Hibiscus grandiflorus.

Drawn from Nature by J.J.Audubon. F.R.S.F.L.S.

Lith.ᵈ Printed & Col.ᵈ by J.T. Bowen. Philad.ᵗ

R.T.

Carbonated Swamp-Warbler
Males
May-bush or Service. Pyrus Botryapium.

Drawn from Nature by J.J.Audubon F.R.S.F.L.S.   Lithd Printed & Cold by J.T.Bowen, Philad.a

R.T.

Golden-winged Swamp-Warbler.

1 Male. 2 Female.

Drawn from Nature by J.J.Audubon. F.R.S.F.L.S.   Lithd Printed & Cold by J.T.Bowen, Philada

R.T.

Nashville Swamp Warbler

1 Male. 2 Female

Swamp Spice   Ilex prinoides

Drawn from Nature by J.J.Audubon. F.R.S.F.L.S.   Lith.d Printed & Col.d by J.T. Bowen. Philad.a

Pl. 112.

Orange-crowned Swamp-Warbler.

1. Male. 2. Female.

Huckleberry. Vaccinium frondosum.

Drawn from Nature by J.J.Audubon.F.R.S.F.L.S.

Lithd. Printed & Cold. by J.T.Bowen.Philadª.

R.T.

Prothonotary Swamp Warbler.

1. Male. 2. Female.

Cane Vine

Drawn from Nature by J.J.Audubon. F.R.S.F.L.S.

Lithᵈ. Printed & Colᵈ by J.T. Bowen, Philadᵃ

Swainson's Swamp Warbler.
Male.
Orange-coloured Azalea. Azalea calendulacea

Drawn from Nature by J.J.Audubon, F.R.S.F.L.S.   Lith⁴ Printed & Col⁴ by J.T.Bowen, Philad⁴

R.T.

Tennessee Swamp Warbler.

Male

Ilex laxiflora

Drawn from Nature by J.J.Audubon,F.R.S.F.L.S.   Lith.ª Printed & Col.ª by J.T.Bowen,Philad.ª

Worm-eating Swamp Warbler.
1. Male. 2. Female.
American Poke-weed. Phytolacca decandra.

Drawn from Nature by J.J. Audubon, F.R.S.F.L.S.   Lithd Printed & Cold by J.T. Bowen. Philad.

R.T.

Black-and-white Creeping Warbler

Male.

Black Larch. Pinus pendula.

Drawn from Nature by J.J. Audubon. F.R.S.F.L.S.

Lith.ᵈ Printed & Col.ᵈ by J.T. Bowen. Philad.ᵃ

2.

1.

Brown Tree-creeper

1 Male 2 Female

Drawn from Nature by J.J.Audubon, F.R.S.F.L.S.   Lith.ᵈ Printed & Col.ᵈ by J.T.Bowen, Philad.ᵃ

Bewicks Wren

Male.

Iron-wood Tree

Drawn from Nature by J.J.Audubon, F.R.S.F.L.S.   Lithd. Printed & Cold. by J.T.Bowen, Philada.

Great Carolina Wren.

1. Male. 2. Female.

Dwarf Buck-eye. Æsculus. Pavia.

Drawn from Nature by J.J.Audubon,F.R.S.F.L.S.   Lith.ᵈ Printed & Col.ᵈ by J. T. Bowen, Philad.ᵃ

Pl. 123.

Marsh Wren

1. Males 2 Female and Nest

Drawn from Nature by J. J. Audubon F.R.S.E.L.S.

Lith? Printed & Col? by J. T. Bowen, Philad?

House Wren

1. Male. 2. Female. 3. Young.
In an old Hat.

Drawn from Nature by J.J.Audubon, F.R.S.F.L.S.   Lith.d Printed & Col.d by J.T.Bowen,Philad.a

Parkman's Wren.

Male.
Pogonia divaricata

Drawn from Nature by J.J. Audubon F.R.S F.L.S.   Lith.d Printed & Col.d by J.T. Bowen Philad.a

Rock - Wren

Adult Female

Smilacina borealis

Drawn from Nature by J.J.Audubon.F.R.S.F.L.S.

Lith⁴ Printed & Col⁴ by J.T. Bowen, Philad⁴

P....T

Short-billed Marsh Wren.

1. Male. 2. Female and Nest.

Drawn from Nature by J.J.Audubon F.R.S.FL.S   Lith! Printed&Col! by J.T.Bowen,Philad!

Pl.121.

Winter Wren.

1. Male. 2. Female. 3. Young.

Drawn from Nature by J.J. Audubon. F.R.S.F.L.S.

Lith⁴ Printed & Col⁴ by J.T. Bowen, Philad⁴

Wood Wren

Male.

Arbutus. Uva-ursi

Drawn from Nature by J.J.Audubon.F.R.S.F.L.S.

Lith⁴ Printed & Col⁴ by J.T.Bowen,Philad⁴

Pl 126.

Black cap Titmouse

1. Male 2 Female

Sweet Brier.

Drawn from Nature by J.J.Audubon F.R.S.F.L.S.

Lith Printed & col.d by J.T.Bowen Phila.r

Pl. 127.

1

2

R.T.

Carolina Titmouse.

1. Male. 2. Female.

Plant. Supple Jack.

Drawn from Nature by J. J. Audubon F.R.S.F.L.S.

Lithd Printed & Cold by J. T. Bowen. Philadª

Chesnut-backed Titmouse.

1. Male. 2. Female.

R. T.

Chesnut-crowned Titmouse

1. Male. 2. Female and Nest.

Drawn from Nature by J.J.Audubon. F.R.S.F.L.S.   Lithd Printed & Cold by J.T. Bowen, Philada

Crested Titmouse

1. Male 2. Female.
White Pine. Pinus Strobus

Drawn from Nature by J. J. Audubon. F.R.S. F.L.S.   Lith⁴ Printed & Col⁴ by J. T. Bowen. Philad⁴.

Hudson's Bay Titmouse.

1. Male. 2. Female. 3. Young.

Drawn. from Nature by J.J. Audubon.F.R.S.F.L.S   Lithᵈ Printed & Colᵈby J.T. Bowen.Philadᵃ

American Golden-crested Kinglet.

1. *Male* 2. *Female*.

Thalia dealbata.

Drawn from Nature by J.J.Audubon.F.R.S.F.L.S.   Lithᵈ Printed & Colᵈ by J.T.Bowen,Philadᵃ

2.F.

Cuvier's Kinglet

Male.

Broad-leaved laurel. Kalmia latifolia.

Drawn from Nature by J.J.Audubon, F.R.S.F.L.S.   Lith. Printed & Col.d by J.T.Bowen, Philad.a

Ruby-crowned Kinglet

1. Male. 2. Female.

Kalmia augustifolia.

Drawn from Nature by J.J.Audubon.F.R.S.F.L.S.   Lithd Printed & Cold by J.T. Bowen Philadª

Arctic Blue Bird
Male 1. Female 2

Drawn from nature by J.J. Audubon F.R.S.F.L.S.   Lith & Printed by Endicott New York.

Common Blue Bird

1. Male. 2. Female. 3 Young.

Great Mullein Verbascum Thapsus.

Drawn from Nature by J.J.Audubon.F.R.S.F.L.S

Lithd Printed & Cold by J.T.Bowen.Philada

Western Blue Bird.

1. *Male.* 2. *Female.*

Drawn from Nature by J.J.Audubon. F.R.S.F.L.S.   Lith.d Printed & Col.d by J.T. Bowen. Philad.a

Pl. 137.

Drawn from nature by J.J. Audubon F.R.S FL.S

Lith. & Printed by Endicott New York

American Dipper.
Male & Female 2.

Pl. 140.

Cat Bird

Male 1 Female 2.

Plant Black-berry , Rubus villosus .

Drawn from nature by J.J. Audubon F.R.S F.L.S.

Lith. & Printed by Endicott New York .

Common Mocking Bird
Males 1 & 2 Female 3,
Florida Jessamine, Gelseminum nitidum
Rattlesnake

Drawn from nature by J.J. Audubon F.R.S.F.L.S.

Lith. & Printed by Endicott New York.

Pl. 141.

Ferruginous Mocking Bird
Males 1.2.3, Female 4.

Drawn from nature by J.J. Audubon F.R.S.F.L.S.   Lith & Printed by Endicott New York.

Mountain Mocking Bird.
Male.

Drawn from nature by J.J. Audubon F.R.S.F.L.S.　　　　Lith. & Printed by Endicott New York.

Pl. 142

American Robin, or Migratory Thrush.
Male 1. Female 2 and young

Chesnut Oak Quercus prinus.

Drawn from nature by J.J. Audubon F.R.S.F.L.S.

Lith. & Printed by Endicott New York

Dwarf Thrush
Male

Plant Porcelia Triloba.

Drawn from nature by J.J. Audubon F.R.S.F.L.S.

Lith. & Printed by Endicott New York.

Hermit Thrush
Male 1. Female 2.
Plant Robin Wood.

Drawn from nature by J.J. Audubon F.R.S.F.L.S.   Lith. & Printed by Endicott New York.

Tawny Thrush,
Male,

Habenaria Lacera — Cornus Canadensis

Drawn from nature by J.J. Audubon F.R.S.F.L.S.   Lith. & Printed by Endicott New York

Varied Thrush.
Male 1, Female 2.
American Mistletoe, Viscum verticillatum.

Drawn from nature by J.J Audubon F.R.S.F.L.S.   Lith. & Printed by Endicott New York.

Wood Thrush
Male 1. Female 2.
Common Dogwood.

Drawn from nature by J.J. Audubon F.R.S.FL.S   Lith & Printed by Endicott New York

Pl.149.

Aquatic Wood - Wagtail
Male 1 Female 2.
Plant. Indian Turnip.

Drawn from nature by J.J Audubon F.R.S.F.L.S.   Lith & Printed by Endicott New York

Golden Crowned Wagtail (Thrush.)
Male 1. Female 2.
Plant Woody Nightshade.

Drawn from nature by J.J. Audubon F.R.S.F.L.S.   Lith. & Printed by Endicott New York

Pl. 150.

American Pipit or Titlark.
Male 1 Female 2.

Drawn from nature by J.J. Audubon F.R.S.F.L.S.

Lith. & Printed by Endicott New York

Shore Lark

PL. 151

Nº 31.

156

1 Male Summer Plumage. 2. Dº Winter. 3 Female. 4 Young & Nest.

Drawn from Nature by J. J. Audubon. F.R.S. F.L.S

Lithᵈ Printed & Colᵈ by J. T. Bowen. Philadᵃ

Pl.486.

N°. 98.

Sprague's Missouri Lark

Male.

Drawn from Nature by J.J.Audubon,F.R.S.F.L.S

Lith Printed & Col.^d by J.T.Bowen Phila.

Pl. 497.

No. 100.

W.E.H.

Western Shore Lark.

Male.

Drawn From Nature by J. J. Audubon, F.R.S. F.L.S.

Lith. Printed & Col.d by J. T. Bowen, Philad.a

R.T.

Chesnut-collared Lark-Bunting.

Male.

Drawn from Nature by J.J.Audubon.F.R.S.F.L.S.   Lithd Printed & Cold by J.T.Bowen.Philadª

Pl.152.

1.

2.

3.

Lapland Lark Bunting.

1. Male Spring Plumage 2. D° Winter: 3. Female.

Drawn from Nature by J.J.Audubon.F.R.S.FL.S.

Lith: Printed & Col⁴ by J.T.Bowen.Philad⁴.

R.T.

Painted Lark-Bunting.

Male.

Drawn from Nature by J.J.Audubon.F.R.S.F.L.S.   Lithd. Printed & Cold. by J.T.Bowen Philadd.

Pl. 487.

Smith's Lark Bunting.
Adult. Male.

Drawn from Nature by J. J. Audubon, F. R. S. F. L. S

Lith. Printed & Col.d by J. T. Bowen, Phila.s

2.5

Snow Lark Bunting

1. 2. Adult. 3. Young.

Drawn from Nature by J.J.Audubon.F.R.S.F.L.S.   Lithd Printed & Cold by J.T.Bowen. Philadª

Baird's Bunting.
Male.

Drawn from Nature by J.J.Audubon FRSFLS

Lith Printed & Col.d by J.T.Bowen Philad.a

R. T.

Bay - winged Bunting.

Male.

Prickly Pear Cactus Opuntia.

Drawn from Nature by J. J. Audubon F.R.S.F.L.S.   Lith.ᵈ Printed & Col.ᵈ by J. T. Bowen Philad.ᵃ

R. S.

Black-throated Bunting.

1. Male 2. Female.

Phalaris arundinacea and Antirrhinum Linaria

Drawn from Nature by J.J.Audubon.F.R.S.F.L.S.   Lith.ᵈ Printed & Col.ᵈ by J.T.Bowen Philad.ᵃ

2.

1.

R.T

Canada Bunting (Tree Sparrow.)

1. Male. 2. Female.

Canadian Barberry.

Drawn from Nature by J.J. Audubon. F.R.S.F.L.S.   Lith.ᵈ Printed & Col.ᵈ by J.T.Bowen. Philad.ᵃ

R.T.

Chipping Bunting.
Male.
Black locust or False Acacia.
Robina pseudacacia.

Drawn from Nature by J.J. Audubon F.R.S.F.L.S.   Lithᵈ Printed & Colᵈ by J.T. Bowen Philadᵃ

R. T.

Clay-coloured Bunting.

Male.

Asclepias tuberosa.

Drawn from Nature by J.J.Audubon. F.R.S.F.L.S.   Lith.ᵈ Printed & Col.ᵈ by J.T.Bowen, Philad.ᵃ

R.T.

Field Bunting.

Male.

Calopogon pulchellus. Brown.

Dwarf Huckle-berry. Vaccinium tenellum.

Drawn from Nature by J.J. Audubon. F.R.S.F.L.S.   Lith.ᵈ Printed & Col.ᵈ by J.T.Bowen.Philad.ᵃ

Shape of tail.

♂

Henslow's Bunting.
Male.
Indian Pink-root or Worm-grass.
Spigelia Marilandica
Phlox   aristata ?

R.T.

Lark Bunting.

Male.

Drawn from Nature by J.J Audubon, F.R.S.F.L.S   Lith.d Printed & Col.d by J T Bowen Philad.a

Le Conti's Sharp-tailed Bunting.

Male.

Drawn from Nature by J.J. Audubon, F.R.S.F.L.S.

Lith Printed & Col.d by J.T. Bowen, Philad.a

R.T.

Savannah Bunting

1. Male. 2. Female.

Indian Pink-root. Spigelia Marilandica.

Drawn from Nature by J.J.Audubon, F.R.S.F.L.S.   Lith.ᵈ Printed & Colᵈ by J.T.Bowen,Philadᵃ

Pl. 493.

Shattucks Bunting

Male

Drawn from Nature by J.J. Audubon, F.R.S.F.L.S.   Lith. Printed & Col by J.T. Bowen, Philad

R.T.

Townsend's Bunting.

Male.

Drawn from Nature by J.J. Audubon. F.R.S. F.L.S.   Lithd. Printed & Cold. by J.T. Bowen, Philada.

R. T.

Yellow-winged Bunting.

Male.

Drawn from Nature by J.J. Audubon. F.R.S.F.L.S.

Lith.ᵈ Printed & Col.ᵈ by J. T. Bowen. Philad.ᵃ

2.

1.

R. T.

Common Snow-Bird.

1. Male 2. Female

Drawn from Nature by J.J. Audubon. F.R.S.E.L.S.   Lithd Printed & Cold by J.T. Bowen. Philad.

R.3.

Oregon Snow Bird

1. Male 2. Female.

Rosa Laevigata

Drawn from Nature by J.J.Audubon.F.R.S.F.L.S.

Lith⁴ Printed & Col⁴ by J.T.Bowen Philad⁴

Indigo Bunting.

1. 2. 3. Males in different States of Plumage. 4. Female.

Wild Sarsaparilla.

Drawn from Nature by J.J.Audubon.F.R.S.F.L.S.   Lithᵈ Printed & Colᵈ by J. T. Bowen, Philadᵃ

R. T.

Lazuli Finch.

1. Male. 2. Female.
♂ *Wild Spanish Coffee.*

Drawn from Nature by J.J. Audubon, F.R.S.F.L.S.

Lith⁴ Printed & Col⁴ by J. T. Bowen, Philad⁴.

Painted Bunting

1. 2. 3. Males in different States of Plumage. 4. Female.
Chicasaw Wild Plum.

Drawn from Nature by J. J. Audubon, F.R.S. F.L.S.

Lith⁴ Printed & Col⁴ by J. T. Bowen Philad⁴

Macgillivray's Shore-Finch.

1. Male. 2. Female.

Drawn from Nature by J. J. Audubon, F.R.S.F.L.S.   Lith.^d Printed & Col.^d by J. T. Bowen, Philad.^a

Pl. 172.

R.T

Sea-side Finch.

1. Male 2. Female

Carolina Rose.

Drawn from Nature by J. J. Audubon F.R.S.F.L.S

Lith.d Printed & Col.d by J. T. Bowen Philad.a

Sharp-tailed Finch.

1. Males. 2. Female & Nest.

Drawn from Nature by J.J. Audubon, F.R.S.F.L.S.   Lith.ᵈ Printed & Col.ᵈ by J.T. Bowen, Philadᵃ

R. T.

Swamp Sparrow
Male.
May-apple

Drawn from Nature by Mrs Lucy Audubon.   Lithd Printed & Cold by J. T. Bowen Philadª

Bachman's Pinewood Finch

Male.

Pinckneya pubescens.

Drawn from Nature by J.J.Audubon.F.R.S.F.L.S.   Lith.d Printed & Col.d by J.T.Bowen.Philad.a

Lincoln's Pinewood Finch.

1. Male. 2. Female.

1. Dwarf Cornel. 2. Cloudberry 3. Glaucous Kalmia.

Drawn from Nature by J.J. Audubon F.R.S.E.L.S.   Lith.d Printed & Col.d by J.T Bowen Philad.

Lesser Redpoll Linnet.

1. Male. 2. Female.

Drawn from Nature by J.J.Audubon F.R.S.E.L.S.   Lithd Printed & Cold by J.T.Bowen Philad.

Pl. 178.

Mealy Redpoll Linnet.

Male.

Drawn from Nature by J.J. Audubon. F.R.S.F.L.S.   Lith.ᵈ Printed & Col.ᵈ by J.T. Bowen. Philad.ᵃ

R.T.

Pine Linnet.

1 Male. 2 Female
Black Larch.

Drawn from Nature by J.J.Audubon. F.R.S.F.L.S.   Lith Printed & Col.d by J.T.Bowen Phila.d

American Goldfinch

1 Male. 2. Female

Common Thistle

Drawn from Nature by J.J. Audubon F.R.S.F.L.S.   Lithd Printed & Cold by J.T. Bowen Philad

Arkansaw Goldfinch.

Male.

Drawn from Nature by J.J. Audubon. F.R.S.F.L.S.   Lith.d Printed & Col.d by J.T. Bowen Philad.

Black-headed Goldfinch.

Male

Drawn from Nature by J.J. Audubon. F.R.S.F.L.S.   Lith.d Printed & Col.d by J.T. Bowen. Philad.

Stanley Goldfinch.

Drawn from Nature by J.J Audubon. F.R.S.F.L.S.   Lithd Printed & Cold by J.T. Bowen Philada

Yarrell's Goldfinch

1 Male. 2. Female.

Drawn from Nature by J.J.Audubon.F.R.S.F.L.S.   Lith.d Printed & Col.d by J.T. Bowen Philad.

Black-and-yellow-crowned Finch.

Drawn from Nature by J.J. Audubon. F.R.S.E.L.S.   Lith.ᵈ Printed & Col.ᵈ by J. T. Bowen. Philad.

Brown Finch

Female

Drawn from Nature by J.J.Audubon.F.R.S.F.L.S.

Pub.d Printed & Col.d by J.T.Bowen Phila.a

Pl. 186.

1.

2.

Fox - coloured Finch.

1. Male. 2. Female.

Drawn from Nature by J.J.Audubon. F.R.S.F.L.S.

Lith.ª Printed & Col.ª by J.T.Bowen. Phila.ª

WEH

Harris' Finch

1. Adult Male. 2. Young Female.

Drawn from Nature by J.J.Audubon, F.R.S.F.L.S.   Lith Printed & Col.ᵈ by J.T.Bowen, Phila.

Pl.189.

Song Finch

1. Male. 2. Female.

Huckle-berry, or Blue tangled Vaccinium frondosum?

Drawn from Nature by J.J.Audubon.F.R.S.F.L.S.   Lithd Printed & Cold by J.T.Bowen.Philad.

Morton's Finch.

Male.

Drawn from Nature by J.J.Audubon.F.R.S.F.L.S.

Lith.ª Printed & Col.ª by J.T.Bowen. Philad.

Pl. 188.

Townsend's Finch

Male.

Drawn from Nature by J.J.Audubon. F.R.S.F.L.S.

Lith.ª Printed & Col.ª by J.T.Bowen, Philad.ª

White-crowned Finch.

1. Male. 2. Female.
Wild Summer Grape.

Drawn from Nature by J.J. Audubon, F.R.S.F.L.S.   Lith. Printed & Col. by J. T. Bowen Philad.

White-throated Finch.

1. *Male.* 2. *Female.*

Common Dogwood.

Drawn from Nature by J.J.Audubon,F.R.S.F.L.S.

Lithᵈ Printed & Colᵈby J. T. Bowen, Philadᵗ

Pl. 194.

1.

2.

R.T.

Arctic Ground Finch.

1. Male. 2. Female.

Drawn from Nature by J.J. Audubon, F.R.S.F.L.S.

Lith. Printed & Col.d by J.T. Bowen, Philad.

Towhe Ground Finch.

1. Male. 2. Female.
Common Blackberry.

Drawn from Nature by J.J. Audubon. F.R.S.F.L.S.   Lithd Printed & Cold by J.T. Bowen Philad.

Crimson-fronted Purple Finch.

Male.

Drawn from Nature by J. J. Audubon. F.R.S.F.L.S.   Lithd Printed & Cold by J. T. Bowen. Philad.

Crested Purple Finch.

1. Males. 2. Female

Red Larch. Larix Americana.

Drawn from Nature by J.J.Audubon,F.R.S.F.L.S.

Lith⁴Printed & Col⁴by J. T. Bowen, Philad⁴

Grey-crowned Purple Finch.

Male.

Stokesia cyanea

Drawn from Nature by J.J.Audubon.F.R.S.F.L.S.

Lith.ᵈ Printed & Col.ᵈ by J.T.Bowen.Philad.

Common Pine-finch.

1.—Male. 2.—Female.

Drawn from Nature by J. J. Audubon, F.R.S.F.L.S.   Lith⁴, Printed & Col⁴ by J. T. Bowen, Phil.

Pl. 200.

Common Crossbill.

1. Males. 2. Females.

Drawn from Nature by J. J. Audubon. F.R.S.F.L.S.

Lith⁴ Printed & Col⁴ by J. T. Bowen. Phil.

212

White-winged Crossbill.

1. Males. 2. Female.

Drawn from Nature by J.J.Audubon,F.R.S.F.L.S.   Lithd Printed & Cold by J. T. Bowen, Philadª

Prairie Lark-Finch.

1. Male. 2. Female.

Drawn from Nature by J.J. Audubon.F.R.S.F.L.S.   Lith.d Printed & Col.d by J.T.Bowen.Philad.

Pl.203.

Common Cardinal Grosbeak.

1. Male. 2. Female.

Wild Almond. Prunus caroliniana.

Drawn from Nature by J.J.Audubon.F.R.S.F.L.S.

Lith.ª Printed & Col.ᵈ by J.T.Bowen Phil.

Pl. 206.

Black-headed Song-Grosbeak.

1. Males 2. Female.

Pl. 204.

Blue Song Grosbeak.

1. Male. 2. Female. 3. Young.

Drawn from Nature by J. J. Audubon. F.R.S.F.L.S.   Lithd Printed & Cold by J. T. Bowen. Philad.

Rose-breasted Song-Grosbeak.
1. Males. 2. Female. 3. Young Male.

Ground Hemlock Taxus canadensis.

Drawn from Nature by J.J.Audubon, F.R.S.F.L.S.

Lith.ª Printed & Col.ª by J. T. Bowen, Philad.ª

Evening Grosbeak.

1. Male. 2. Female. 3. Young Male.

Drawn from Nature by J.J. Audubon. F.R.S.F.L.S.

Lith.ᵈ Printed & Col.ᵈ by J. T. Bowen Philad.

Louisiana Tanager.

1. Males. 2. Female.

Drawn from Nature by J.J.Audubon,F.R.S.F.L.S.

Lith.ᵈPrinted & Col.ᵈby J. T. Bowen, Philad.ᵈ

1.

2.

Scarlet Tanager.

1. Male. 2. Female.

Drawn from Nature by J.J.Audubon. F.R.S.F.L.S.   Lith.ª Printed & Col.ª by J.T.Bowen, Philad.

Summer Red-bird

1. Male. 2. Female 3. Young Male.

Wild Muscadine Vitis rotundifolia. Mich

Drawn from Nature by J.J.Audubon,F.R.S.F.L.S.   Lith.¹Printed & Col.¹by J.T.Bowen, Philad.ª

Pl. 211.

Wandering Rice-bird

1 Male. 2 Female

Red Maple. Acer Rubrum.

Drawn from Nature by J.J. Audubon. F.R.S.F.L.S.   Lith.ᵈ Printed & Col.ᵈ by J. T. Bowen Philad.

Pl. 212.

3

1

2

Common Cow-bird.

1. Male. 2. Female. 3. Young.

Drawn from Nature by J.J.Audubon.F.R.S.F.L.S.

Lith.ᵈ Printed & Col.ᵈ by J.T.Bowen, Philad.

Red-and-black-shouldered Marsh-Blackbird

1. Male 2. Female.

Drawn from Nature by J.J.Audubon.F.R.S.F.L.S.   Lithᵈ Printed & Colᵈ by J.T.Bowen Philad

Red-and-white-shouldered. Marsh Blackbird

Male.

Drawn from Nature by J.J. Audubon. F.R.S.F.L.S.   Lithd Printed & Cold by J.T. Bowen Philad.

Red-winged Starling

1. Male Adult. 2. Young Male. 3. Female.

Red Maple

Drawn from Nature by J.J. Audubon. F.R.S.F.L.S.   Lithd. Printed & Cold. by J. T. Bowen. Philad.

Pl 213.

Saffron-headed Marsh-Blackbird.

1. Male. 2. Female 3. Young Male.

Drawn from Nature by J. J. Audubon. F.R.S.F.L.S.

Lith.d Printed & Col.d by J.T. Bowen. Philad.

Pl. 217.

Baltimore Oriole, or Hang-nest

1 Male adult. 2 Young Male. 3 Female.

Tulip Tree.

Drawn from Nature by J. J. Audubon. F.R.S.F.L.S.

Lith.ᵈ Printed & Col.ᵈ by J. T. Bowen. Phil.ᵃ

Pl. 218.

Bullock's Troopial

1. Male Adult. 2. Young Male. 3. Female

Caprifolium flavum.

Drawn from Nature by J.J. Audubon. F.R.S.F.L.S.

Lithd Printed & Cold by J. T. Bowen Phil.

Common Troupial.

Male.

Drawn from Nature by J.J.Audubon,F.R.S.F.L.S.   Lith^d.Printed & Col^d.by J. T. Bowen, Philad^a.

Pl 219.

Orchard Oriole or Hang-nest.

1. Male adult. 2. Young Male. 3. Female & Nest.

Honey Locust.

Drawn from Nature by J.J.Audubon. F.R.S.F.L.S.

Lith.d Printed & Col.d by T Bowen, Phil.

Boat-tailed Grackle.

1. Male. 2. Female.

Live Oak.

Drawn from Nature by J.J.Audubon. F.R.S.F.L.S   Lith.ᵈ Printed & Col.ᵈ by J.T.Bowen.Phil.

R.T.

Brewers Black-bird.

Male.

Drawn from Nature by J.J.Audubon F.R.S.F.L.S.

Lith Printed & Col.d by J.T.Bowen, Philad.a

Common or Purple Crow Blackbird.

1. Male. 2. Female.

Maize or Indian Corn.

Drawn from Nature by J. J. Audubon, F.R.S.F.L.S.   Lith.ª Printed & Col.ª by J. T. Bowen. Philad.

Pl222.

Rusty Crow-Blackbird.

1 Male. 2 Female. 3 Young.
Black Haw.

Drawn from Nature by J.J. Audubon F.R.S.F.L.S.   Lith⁴ Printed & Col⁴ by J. T. Bowen Philad.

Meadow Starling or Meadow Lark.
1. *Males.* 2. *Female and Nest.*
Yellow flowered Gerardia.

Drawn from Nature by J.J.Audubon,F.R.S.F.L.S.   Lithd Printed & Cold by J. T. Bowen, Philad.ª

W.E.H.

Missouri Meadow Lark.

Male

Drawn from Nature by J.J.Audubon, F.R.S.FL.S.

Lith Printed & Col.d by J.T.Bowen, Philad.a

Common American Crow

Male.

Black Walnut

Drawn from Nature by J.J.Audubon. F.R.S.F.L.S

Lith.d Printed & Col.d by J.T.Bowen. Phil

Fish Crow.

1 Male. 2 Female.

Honey Locust.

Drawn from Nature by J. J. Audubon F.R.S.F.L.S.

Lith. Printed & Col. by J. T. Bowen Phil.

Raven

Old Male.

Thick-Shell, bark Hickory

Drawn from Nature by J.J.Audubon.F.R.S.F.L.S.   Lith.ᵈPrinted & Colᵈby J.T.Bowen.Philad

Columbia Magpie or Jay.
Males

Drawn from Nature by J. J. Audubon. F. R. S. F. L. S.   Lithd. Printed & Cold. by J. T. Bowen, Phil.

1.

2.

Common Magpie.

1. Male 2. Female.

Drawn from Nature by J.J.Audubon.F.R.S.F.L.S.   Lith.ᵈ Printed & Col.ᵈ by J.T.Bowen Philad.

Pl. 228.

Yellow-billed Magpie.

Male.

Plantanus.

Drawn from Nature by J. J. Audubon F.R.S.F.L.S   Lith.ᵈ Printed & Col.ᵈ by J. T. Bowen Philad.

Blue Jay

1. Male. 2 & 3. Female

Trumpet flower. Bignonia radicans.

Drawn from Nature by J.J. Audubon. F.R.S. F.L.S.   Lithd. Printed & Cold by J.T. Bowen. Philad.

Pl. 234

Canada Jay

1. Male. 2. Female. 3. Young
White Oak. Quercus alba.

Drawn from Nature by J.J.Audubon. F.R.S.F.L.S.

Lith⁴.Printed & Col⁴.by J.T.Bowen. Phil.

Florida Jay

1. Male ---2. Female.

Persimontree. Diospyros Virginiana.

Drawn from Nature by J.J.Audubon.F.R.S.F.L.S.   Lithᵈ Printed & Colᵈ by J.T.Bowen.Phil.

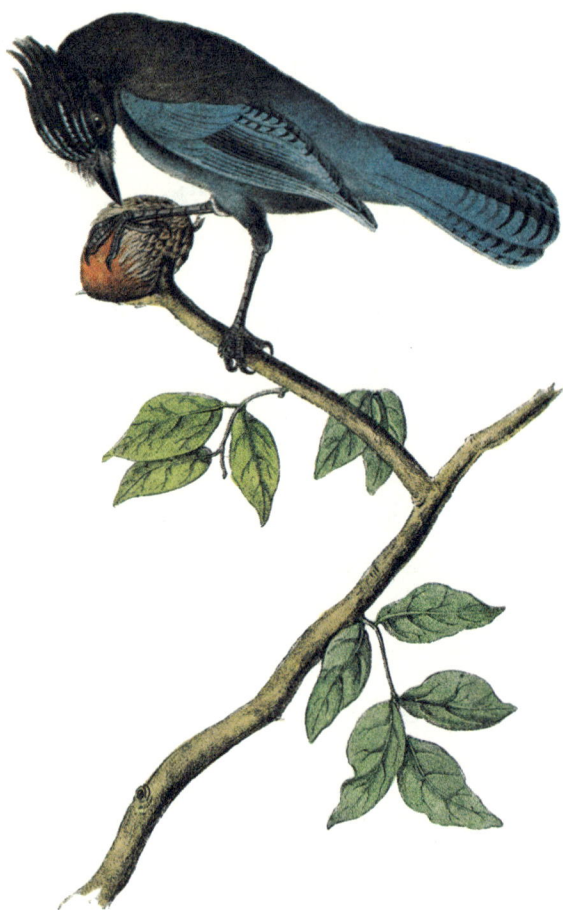

R.T.

Stellers Jay

. Male.

Drawn from Nature by J.J. Audubon F.R.S.F.L.S.   Lith.d Printed & Col.d by J.T. Bowen Phil.a

Pl. 232.

Ultramarine Jay

Adult Male.

Drawn from Nature by J.J.Audubon.F.R.S.F.L.S.   Lith.d Printed & Col.d by J.T Bowen.Phil.

Pl. 235.

Clarke's Nutcracker.

1. Male. 2. Female.

Drawn from Nature by J.J. Audubon, F.R.S.F.L.S

Lith Printed & Col.d by J.T. Bowen, Phil.a

Great American Shrike.

1. Male. 2. Female. 3. Young.
Crataegus Apiifolia.

Drawn from Nature by J.J.Audubon, F.R.S.F.L.S.   Lith⁴ Printed & Col⁴ by J. T. Bowen. Phil.

R.T.
Loggerhead Shrike

1. Male. 2. Female.

Greenbriar or Round-leaved Smilax. Smilax Rotundifolia

Drawn from Nature by J.J.Audubon.F.R.S.F.L.S.   Lith.ᵈ Printed & Col.ᵈ by J. T. Bowen. Philad.

Bartrams Vireo or Greenlet

Male
Ipomea

Drawn from Nature by J.J.Audubon. F.R.S.F.L.S.   Lithᵈ Printed & Colᵈ by J. T. Bowen. Phil.

Pl. 485.

Bell's Vireo.

Male.

Rattle-snake Root

Drawn from Nature by J.J.Audubon, F.R.S.F.L.S.   Lith. Printed & Col.d by J.T.Bowen, Phila.

Pl. 243.

n.5

Red-eyed Vireo or Greenlet.

Male.
Honey-locust.

Drawn from Nature by J.J.Audubon. F.R.S.F.L.S.   Lith^d. Printed & Col^d. by J. T. Bowen. Phil.

Solitary Vireo or Greenlet.
1 Male. 2 Female.

American Cane. *Miegia macrosperma*.

Drawn from Nature by J.J. Audubon, F.R.S.E.L.S.   Lith.ᵈ Printed & Col.ᵈ by J.T. Bowen Phil.

Pl. 241.

Warbling Vireo or Greenlet

1 Male. 2. Female.
Swamp Magnolia

Drawn from Nature by J.J. Audubon. F.R.S.F.L.S.   Lith.d Printed & Col.d by J.T. Bowen. Philad.

White-eyed Vireo, or Greenlet.

Male.

Pride of China, or bead tree. Melia Azedarach.

Drawn from Nature by J.J. Audubon. F.R.S.F.L.S.

Lith.ᵈ Printed & Col.ᵈ by J. T. Bowen. Phil.ᵃ

B.T.

Yellow-throated Vireo, or Greenlet.

Male.

Swamp Snowball. Hydraugea quercifolia.

Drawn from Nature by J.J.Audubon.F.R.S.F.L.S.   Lith.ᵈPrinted & Col.ᵈ by J.T.Bowen.Philad

Pl. 244.

Yellow-breasted Chat.

1. 2. 3. *Male* 4. *Female.*
Sweet briar.

Drawn from Nature by J.J. Audubon. F.R.S. F.L.S.   Lith.d Printed & Col.d by J. T. Bowen, Phil.

Black throated Wax-wing.
or Bohemian Chatterer.
1. Male. 2. Female.
Canadian Service Tree.

Drawn from Nature by J.J.Audubon.F.R.S.F.L.S.   Lithd Printed & Cold by J.T.Bowen.Philad

Cedar bird, or Cedar Wax-wing

1. Male 2. Female.

Red Cedar.

Drawn from Nature by J.J. Audubon. F.R.S.F.L.S   Lithd Printed & Cold by J.T. Bowen. Philad.

Pl. 249.

Brown-headed Nuthatch

1. *Male.* 2. *Female.*

Drawn from Nature by J.J. Audubon. F.R.S. F.L.S.   Lith.ᵈ Printed & Col.ᵈ by J. T. Bowen. Phil.

Californian Nuthatch.

Adults.

Drawn from Nature by J.J. Audubon F.R.S.F.L.S.   Lith.ᵈ Printed & Col.ᵈ by J.T. Bowen Phil.

Pl. 248.

Red-bellied Nuthatch

1. Male 2. Female.

Drawn from Nature by J.J. Audubon, F.R.S.F.L.S.   Lith^d. Printed & Col^d by J.T. Bowen, Phil.

White-breasted Nuthatch.

1. Male. 2 & 3. Female.

Drawn from Nature by J.J.Audubon.F.R.S.F.L.S.   Lith.ᵈ Printed & Col.ᵈ by J. T. Bowen Phil.

Anna Humming bird.

1. 2. Males. 3 Female.

Hibiscus Virginicus.

Drawn from Nature by J.J.Audubon,F.R.S.F.L.S.   Lith^d Printed & Col^d by J.T.Bowen, Philad^a

Pl. 251.

Mango Humming bird

1. 2. *Males.* 3. *Female*

Bignonia grandifolia.

Drawn from Nature by J.J. Audubon. F.R.S.F.L.S.   Lith.ᵈ Printed & Col.ᵈ by J.T. Bowen. Phil.

Ruby-throated Hummingbird

1. 2. *Males*. 3. *Female*. 4 *Young*

(*Bignonia - radicans*)

Drawn from Nature by J. J. Audubon. F.R.S.F.L.S.   Lith. Printed & Col.d by J. T. Bowen Phil.

Ruff-necked Humming bird.

1. 2. Males. 3. Female.
Cleome heptaphylla.

Drawn from Nature by J.J. Audubon. F.R.S.F.L.S.　　　Lith⁴ Printed & Col⁴ by J.T. Bowen. Phil.

W. H.

Belted Kingfisher

Alcedo Alcyon.

1. Males 2. Female

Drawn from Nature by J.J. Audubon. F.R.S.F.L.S.   Lith.ᵈ Printed & Col.ᵈ by J.T. Bowen. Phil.

Pl. 268.

Arctic three-toed Woodpecker.

1. 2. *Males.* 3. *Female.*

Drawn from Nature by J.J.Audubon. F.R.S.F.L.S.

Lith.d Printed & Col.d by J. T. Bowen. Phil.

A.V.

Audubon's Woodpecker.

Male.

Drawn from Nature by J.J. Audubon F.R.S.F.L.S.   Lith. Printed & Col.d by J.T. Bowen, Phil.

Banded three-toed Woodpecker.

1. Male 2. Female.

Drawn from Nature by J. J. Audubon. F.R.S.F.L.S.

W.H.

Canadian Woodpecker.

Male.

Drawn from Nature by J.J.Audubon.F.R.S.F.L.S   Lith.ᵈ Printed & Col.ᵈ by J.T.Bowen.Phil.

Downy Woodpecker

1. Male. 2. Female.

Drawn from Nature by J. J. Audubon, F.R.S.F.L.S.

Nº.3ª Printed & Col.ª by J. T. Bowen. Phil.

Pl. 273.

A.V.

Golden-winged Woodpecker

1. Male. 2. Females.

Drawn from Nature by J.J. Audubon. F.R.S.F.L.S.

Lithᵈ Printed & Colᵈ by J.T. Bowen. Phil.

Pl. 262.

1.

2.

Hairy Woodpecker.

1. Male 2. Female

Drawn from Nature by J.J. Audubon, F.R.S. F.L.S.

Lith.ᵈ Printed & Col.ᵈ by J.T. Bowen, Phil.

Pl. 261.

1.

2.

J.C

Harris's Woodpecker

1. Male. 2. Female.

Drawn from Nature by J. J. Audubon. F.R.S.F.L.S.

Lith.ᵈ Printed & Col.ᵈ by J. T. Bowen, Phil.

Pl 256.

Ivory-billed Woodpecker.

1 Male. 2 & 3 Female.

Drawn from Nature by J.J.Audubon F.R.S.F.L.S.   Lithᵈ Printed & Colᵈ by J.T.Bowen. Phil.

Lewis' Woodpecker.
1. Male 2. Female

Drawn from Nature by J.J.Audubon.FRS.FLS.   Lithd.Printed & Cold by J.T.Bowen Phil.

Maria's Woodpecker.

1. Male. 2. Female.

Drawn from Nature by J.J.Audubon.F.R.S.F.L.S.   Lith⁴ Printed & Col⁴ by J.T.Bowen,Phil.

WEH.

Missouri Red-moustached Woodpecker

Male

Drawn from Nature by J.J.Audubon,F.R.S.F.L.S   Lith Printed & Col.d by J.T.Bowen,Philad.ª

Phillips' Woodpecker!

Males.

Drawn from Nature by J.J.Audubon.F.R.S.F.L.S.   Lith.ᵈ Printed & Col.ᵈ by J.T. Bowen Phil.

Pl. 257.

Pileated Woodpecker

1. Adult Male. 2. Adult Female. 3 and 4. Young Males.

Raccoon Grape.

Drawn from Nature by J.J.Audubon, F.R.S.E.L.S.

Lith.ᵈ Printed & Col.ᵈ by J. T. Bowen, Phil.

W.H.

Red-bellied Woodpecker.
1. Male. 2. Female.

Drawn from Nature by J.J.Audubon.F.R.S.F.L.S.   Lith.d Printed & Col.d by J.T. Bowen. Phil.

A. V.

Red-breasted Woodpecker.

1. Male. 2. Female.

Drawn from Nature by J.J.Audubon. F.R.S.F.L.S.   Lith. Printed & Col.d by J.T. Bowen. Phil.

Red-cockaded Woodpecker.
1. 2. Males 3. Female.

Drawn from Nature by J.J. Audubon.F.R.S.F.L.S.   Lith.ᵈ Printed & Col.ᵈ by J.T. Bowen, Phil.

Red-headed Woodpecker.

1. Male. 2. Female. 3. Young.

Drawn from Nature by J.J.Audubon, F.R.S.F.L.S.   Lith⁴ Printed & Col⁴ by J. T. Bowen, Philad⁴.

Red-shafted Woodpecker.

1. Male. 2. Female.

Drawn from Nature by J.J.Audubon.F.R.S.F.L.S.   Lith.& Printed & Col.d by J.T.Bowen.Phil.

Yellow-bellied Woodpecker.

1. Male. 2. Female.

Prunus Caroliniana.

Drawn from Nature by J.J. Audubon. F.R.S.E.L.S.   Lithd. Printed & Cold. by J.T. Bowen Phil.

PL276

Nº 56

Black-billed Cuckoo.
1 Male 2 Female.
Magnolia grandiflora.

Drawn from Nature by J.J.Audubon.F.R.S.F.L.S.

Lith Printed & Cold by J. T. Bowen, Phil.

W.H.

Mangrove Cuckoo.

Male.
Seven years apple.

Drawn from Nature by J.J.Audubon.F.R.S.F.L.S   Lithd. Printed & Cold by J.T.Bowen Phil.

Pl. 275.

N°. 55

Yellow-billed Cuckoo
1. Male 2. Female.
Papaw Tree.

Drawn from Nature by J.J.Audubon.F.R.S.F.L.S.

Lith⁴ Printed & Col⁴ by J.T.Bowen.Phil.

W.H.

Carolina Parrot or Parrakeet

1.2. Males . 3. Female. 4. Young.
Cockle bur.

Drawn from Nature by J.J. Audubon F.R.S.F.L.S.   Lithd Printed & Cold by J.T.Bowen. Phil.

Band-tailed Dove or Pigeon.

1. Male. 2. Female.

Cornus nuttalli

Drawn from Nature by J.J. Audubon, F.R.S.E.L.S.   Lith.d Printed & Col.d by J.T. Bowen Phil.

No. 57.

Pl. 284.

1.

2.

Blue-headed Ground Dove or Pigeon

1. Male. 2. Females.

Drawn from Nature by J.J.Audubon.F.R.S.F.L.S.

Lith.Printed & Col.by J. T. Bowen. Phil.

Pl. 283.

Ground Dove.

1. & 2. *Males.* 3. *Female.* 4. *Young*
Wild Orange.

Drawn from Nature by J.J. Audubon F.R.S.F.L.S.   Lith.ᵈ Printed & Col.ᵈ by J. T. Bowen. Phil.

Pl 282.

Key-West Dove

1. Male. 2. Female.

Drawn from Nature by J.J.Audubon. F.R.S.F.L.S.

Lith.ᵈ Printed & Col.ᵈ by J.T.Bowen Philad.

Pl. 496.

The Texan Turtle Dove.

Male.

Drawn from Nature by J. J. Audubon, F.R.S. F.L.S.   Lith Printed & Col.d by J. T. Bowen, Philad.a

A.V.

White-headed Dove, or Pigeon

1. Male. 2. Female.

Cordia sebestina.

Drawn from Nature by J.J.Audubon.F.R.S.F.L.S.   Lithd.Printed & Cold.by J.T.Bowen.Phil.

Zenaida Dove.

1. Male. 2. Female
Anona.

Drawn from Nature by J.J. Audubon, F.R.S.F.L.S.

Lith.ᵈ Printed & Col.ᵈ by J. T. Bowen. Philad.

Passenger Pigeon

1. Male 2. Female.

Drawn from Nature by J.J.Audubon F.R.S.F.L.S.   Lithᵈ Printed & Colᵈ by J.T. Bowen Philᵈ

Pl. 286.

Carolina Turtle Dove.

1. Males 2. Females.

White flowered Stuartia. Stuartia Malacodendron.

Drawn from Nature by J. J. Audubon, F.R.S.F.L.S.

Lithd Printed & Cold by J. T. Bowen, Philadª

Pl. 288.

N° 58.

Wild Turkey.

Female & Young.

Drawn from Nature by J.J.Audubon.FRSFLS.

Lith.d Printed & Col.d by J.T.Bowen. Philad.a

Pl. 2 87

J.C.

Wild Turkey
Male.

Drawn from Nature by J.J.Audubon. F.R.S.F.L.S.

Lith? Printed & Col? by J.T.Bowen.Phil

Pl. 289.

Common American Partridge.

Drawn from Nature by J.J.Audubon,FRSFLS.

1.Male. 2.Female. 3.Young.

Lith'.Printed & Col'.by J.T.Bowen, Phil.d

Pl 290.

1.

2.

Californian Partridge

1. Male. 2. Female.

Drawn from Nature by J.J.Audubon.F.R.S.F.L.S.

Lith Printed. & Col.d by J.T.Bowen Phil.

Pl. 291.

Plumed Partridge.
1. Male. 2. Female.

Drawn from Nature by J.J.Audubon.F.R.S.F.L.S.

PL 292.

Welcome Partridge
Young

Drawn from Nature by J.J. Audubon, F.R.S.F.L.S.
Lith.d Printed & Col.d by J.T.Bowen, Phil.

Pl 294.

Canada Grouse.

1.2. Males. 3. Female.
4. Fulvous [pictum]. 5 [Fraxilops dictorius].

Drawn from Nature by J.J.Audubon. F.R.S.F.L.S.

Lith.d Printed & Col.d by J.T.Bowen. Phil.

Pl 297.

N° 60.

Cock of the Plains.
N°.56
1. Male. 2. Female

Drawn from Nature by J. J. Audubon F.R.S.F.L.S

Lith. Printed & Col.? by J. T. Bowen, Phil.

312

Pl.295.

Dusky Grouse.
1. Male. 2. Female.

Drawn from Nature by J.J.Audubon. F.R.S.F.L.S.

Lith⁴.Printed & Col⁴.by J.T.Bowen.Phila⁴.

Pl. 296.

Pinated Grouse.

1.2. Males. 3 Female. Lilium Superbum.

Drawn from Nature by J.J.Audubon,F.R.S.F.L.S.

Lith.dPrinted & Col.d by J.T.Bowen, Philad.a

Pl 293.

Ruffed Grouse.
1. 2. Males . 3 Females.

Drawn from Nature by J.J.Audubon, F.R.S.E.S

Lith.ª Printed & Col.ª by J. T. Bowen, Philad.ª

Pl 298.

W.H. Sharp-tailed Grouse.

1. Male. 2. Female.

Drawn from Nature by J.J.Audubon, F.R.S.F.L.S.

Lith. Printed & Col. by J.T.Bowen, Phil.

Pl 300.

Drawn from Nature by J.J.Audubon.FRSFLS

56. American Ptarmigan.
Male.

Lith.Printed & Col.d by J.T.Bowen,Phil.a

N°. 61. 2 1. Pl. 301.

3

Rock Ptarmigan

1 Male, in Winter. 2 Female, Summer Plumage/. 3 Young in August.

Drawn from Nature by J.J.Audubon.F.R.S.F.L.S.

Lith.d Printed & Col.d. by J.T.Bowen, Philad.

Pl. 302.

White-tailed Ptarmigan
Adults, in Winter Plumage.

♂ ♀

Drawn from Nature by J.J.Audubon.FRS.FLS.

Lith:&Printed & Col:d by J.T.Bowen,Philad.

Willow — Ptarmigan ?.
1. Male. 2. Female & Young.

Drawn from Nature by J.J.Audubon.F.R.S.F.L.S.

Lith & Printed & Cold by J.T.Bowen.Phil.

Pl 304.

N°. 76.

Common Gallinule.
Adult Male.

Drawn from Nature by J.J.Audubon. F.R.S.F.L.S

Lith Printed & Col.d by J.T.Bowen, Philad.a

Pl. 303.

Purple Gallinule
Adult Male. Spring Plumage

Drawn from Nature by J.J. Audubon. F.R.S.F.L.S.

Lith.d Printed & Col.d by J.T.Bowen, Phil.

PL 305.

Drawn from Nature by J.J.Audubon. F.R.S.F.L.S

American Coot.

Lith⁴.Printed & Col⁴.by J.T.Bowen.Philad⁴.

No. 62.

Pl. 308.

Least Water-Rail.
1. Adult Male. 2. Young.

Drawn from Nature by J.J.Audubon.F.R.S.F.L.S.

Lith.&.Printed & Col.d by J.T.Bowen,Phil.a

Pl. 306.

N°. 62.

Sora Rail.
1 Male. — 2 Female. 3 Young.

Drawn from Nature by J. J. Audubon, F. R. S. F. L. S.

Lith. Printed & Col.d by J. T. Bowen, Philad.a

325

Pl. 307.

Yellow-breasted Rail.
Adult Male in Spring.

Drawn from Nature by J. J. Audubon. F.R.S.F.L.S.

Lith.ᵈ Printed & Col.ᵈ by J. T. Bowen, Phil.

Clapper Rail or Salt Water Marsh Hen!

1. Male. 2. Female.

Drawn from Nature by J.J.Audubon.FRS.FLS.

Lith.d Printed & Col.d by J.T.Bowen. Phil.

Pl 309.

Great Red-breasted Rail or fresh-water Marsh Hen.

1. Male adult. 2. Young.

Drawn from Nature by J. J. Audubon. F. R. S. F. L. S.

Lith.d Print.d & Col.d by J. T. Bowen. Phil.d

Pl.311.

No.63

Virginian Rail
1.Male. 2.Female. 3.Young

Drawn from Nature by J.J.Audubon.F.R.S.F.L.S.

Lith. Printed & Col.d By J.T.Bowen. Phil.

Pl. 312.

Scolopaceus Courlan.

Drawn from Nature by J.J.Audubon.F.R.S.F.L.S.

Lith.& Printed & Col.d by J.T.Bowen, Phil.

Whooping Crane.

Male, adult.

Drawn from Nature by J.J.Audubon,F.R.S.F.L.S.   Lithᵈ Printed & Colᵈ by J. T. Bowen, Philadᵃ

Whooping Crane
Young.

Drawn from Nature by J.J.Audubon.F.R.S.F.L.S.

Lithd Printed & Cold by J. T. Bowen. Phil.

Pl. 316.

Nº 64.

American Golden Plover.
1. Summer Plumage. 2. Winter. 3. Variety in March.

Drawn from Nature by J.J.Audubon.F.R.S.F.L.S.

Tath.Printed & Col.d by J.T.Bowen.Phil.

333

Pl. 320.

2

1

American Ring Plover.
1. Adult Male. 2. Young in August.

Drawn from Nature by J.J.Audubon.F.R.S.F.L.S.

Lith.d. Printed & Col.d by J.T.Bowen,Phil.

Pl. 315.

Black-bellied Plover.

1. Male. 2. Young in Autumn. 3. Nestling.

Drawn from Nature by J.J.Audubon.F.R.S.F.L.S.

Lith.ᵈ Printed & Col.ᵈ by J. T. Bowen, Phil.

Pl. 317.

Kildeer Plover

1. Male. 2. Female.

Drawn from Nature by J.J.Audubon. FRS.FLS.

Lith.d Printed & Cold by J.T.Bowen. Phil.

Pl. 321.

N° 65

Piping Plover.
1. Male. 2. Female.

Drawn from Nature by J.J.Audubon.F.R.S.F.L.S.

Lith.d.Printed & Col.d by J.T.Bowen.Phil.

Pl. 318.

Drawn from Nature by J.J.Audubon, F.R.S.F.L.S

Fig.

Rocky Mountain Plover.

Female.

Lith.ᵈ Printed & Col.ᵈ by J.T. Bowen, Phil.

Pl. 319.

Wilson's Plover.
1. Male. 2. Female.

Drawn from Nature by J.J.Audubon. F.R.S.F.L.S.

Lith. Printed & Col.d by J.T.Bowen, Phil.

Pl. 322.

No. 65.

Townsend's Surf-Bird.
Female.

Drawn from Nature by J.J.Audubon.F.R.S.F.L.S.

Lith.d.Printed & Col.d by J.T.Bowen.Phil.

340

Pl 323.

Drawn from Nature by J.J.Audubon. F.R.S.F.L.S.

Lith.ᵈPrinted & Col.ᵈby J.T.Bowen.Phil

Turnstone. 1. Summer Plumage. 2. Winter.

Pl 324

American Oyster-Catcher.
R.F.
Male.

Drawn from Nature by J.J.Audubon,F.R.S.F.L.S

Lith&Printed & Col.d by J.T.Bowen,Phil.

Pl. 325

Bachman's Oyster-catcher.
Male.

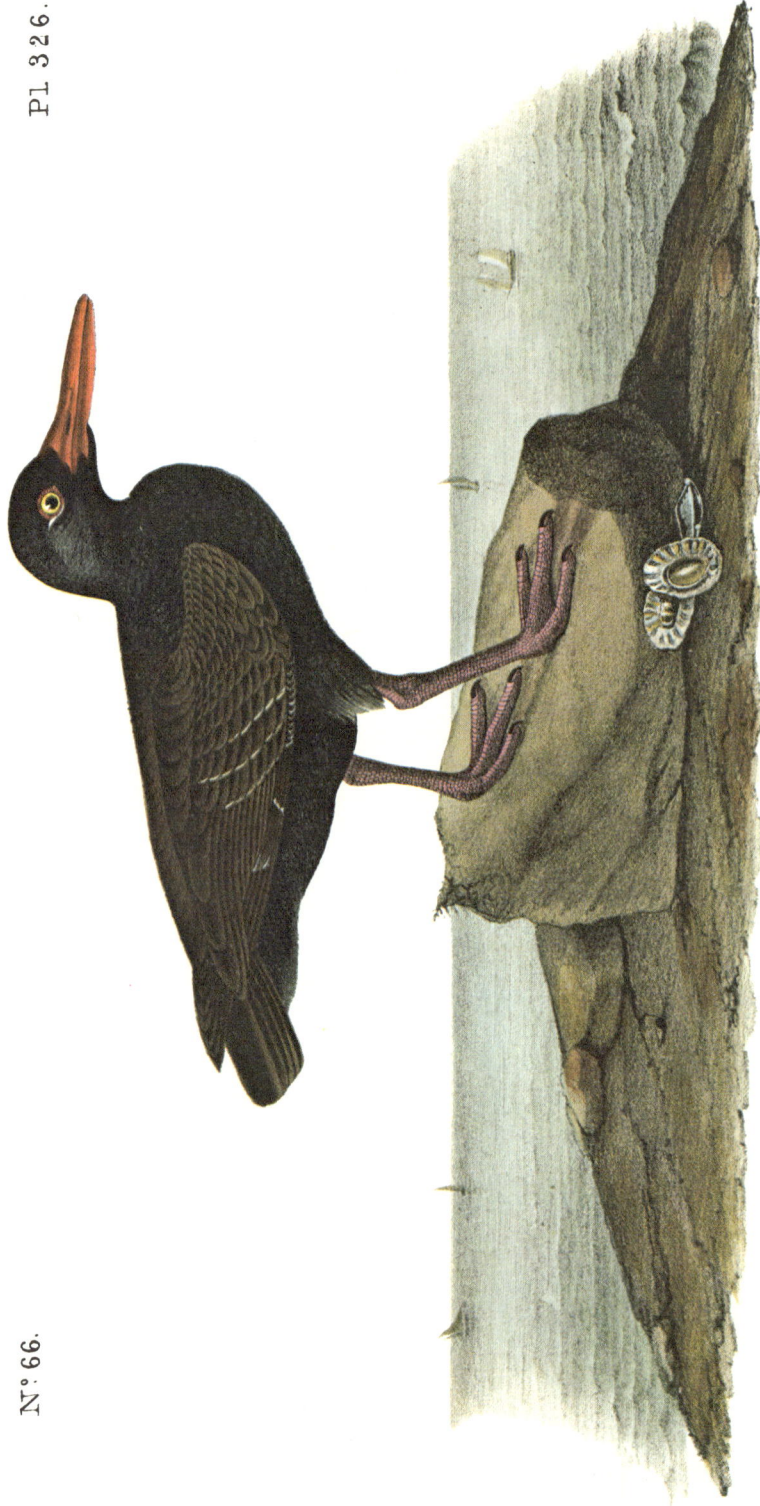

Pl 326.

Townsend's Oyster-catcher.
Female.

Drawn From Nature by J.J.Audubon.F.R.S.F.L.S.

Lith.d Printed & Col.d by J.T.Bowen. Phil.

No. 66.

Pl. 327.

Bartramian Sandpiper

1. Male. 2. Female.

Drawn from Nature by J.J. Audubon. F.R.S.F.L.S.

Lith⁴ Printed & Col⁴ by J.T. Bowen, Phil.

Pl. 331.

Buff=breasted Sand=piper.
1. Male. 2. Female.

Drawn from Nature by J.J.Audubon. F.R.S.F.L.S

Lith⁴.Printed & Col⁴.by J.T.Bowen.Philad⁴.

Pl. 333.

Curlew Sandpiper.
1. Adult Male. 2. Young.

Drawn from Nature by J.J. Audubon. F.R.S.F.L.S.

Lith. Printed & Col.d by J.T. Bowen. Phil.

PL.337.

Little Sandpiper.
1. Male. Summer plumage. 2. Female.

Drawn from Nature by J.J. Audubon. F.R.S.M.S.

Lith. Printed & Cold by J. T. Bowen. Phil.

Pl. 334.

Long-legged Sandpiper.

Drawn from Nature by J.J. Audubon, F.R.S.F.L.S.

Lith.d Printed & Col.d by J.T.Bowen, Phil.

Pl. 329.

1

2.

Pectoral Sandpiper

1. Male. 2. Female.

Drawn from Nature by J. J. Audubon. F.R.S. F.L.S.

Lith. Printed & Col.d by J. T. Bowen. Phil.

N.° 66.

Pl. 330.

2.

1.

Purple Sandpiper.
1. Summer. 2. Winter.

Drawn from Nature by J.J. Audubon, F.R.S.F.L.S.

Lith.& Printed & Col.d by J.T.Bowen, Phil.

Pl. 332.

2.

Red-backed Sandpiper

1. Summer Plumage.—2. Winter.

Drawn from Nature by J.J.Audubon. F.R.S.Ł.S.

Lith.ᵈ Printed & Col.ᵈ by J.T. Bowen, Phil.ᵃ

Pl. 328.

Red-breasted Sandpiper.

1. Summer Plumage. 2 Winter.

Drawn from Nature by J.J.Audubon. F.R.S.F.L.S.

Lith.ᵈ Printed & Col.ᵈ by J. T. Bowen. Phil.

Sanderling Sandpiper.
1. Winter plumage. 2. Summer.

Drawn from Nature by J.J. Audubon. F.R.S.E.F.L.S.

Lith. Printed & Col.d by J.T. Bowen, Phil.

Pl. 335.

N°. 67.

Schinz's Sandpiper
1. Male. 2. Female.

Drawn from Nature by J. J. Audubon. F.R.S.F.L.S.

Lith. & Printed & Col.d by J. T. Bowen, Phila.

355

Pl. 336.

Semipalmated Sandpiper.
1. Summer Plumage. 2. Winter.

Drawn from Nature by J.J. Audubon. F.R.S. F.L.S

Lith. Printed & Col.d by J.T. Bowen, Phila.

PL. 339.

N°. 68.

Red Phalarope

1. Adult Male. 2. Winter plumage.

Drawn from Nature by J.J. Audubon. F.R.S. F.L.S

Lith⁴ Printed & Col⁴ by J. T. Bowen, Philad.

357

Pl 340.

3

2

1

Hyperborean Phalarope.
1. *Male.* 2. *Female.* 3. *Young in autumn.*

Drawn from Nature by J.J.Audubon.F.R.S.F.L.S.

Lith.d Printed & Col.d by J.T.Bowen.Phil.

No. 69.

Pl. 341.

W. H.

Wilsons Phalarope.
1, Male. 2, Female.

Drawn from Nature by J. J. Audubon, F.R.S. F.L.S.

Lith & Printed & Col.d by J. T. Bowen, Phila.

359

Greenshank
Male.
VIEW OF St AUGUSTINE & SPANISH FORT FLORIDA.

Drawn from Nature by J.J. Audubon, F.R.S. F.L.S.

Lith.d Printed & Col.d by J.T.Bowen, Phila.

Pl. 347.

Nº 70.

W.H.

Semipalmated Snipe Willet or Stone Curlew.

1. Male Spring Plumage. 2. Female in Winter.

Drawn from Nature by J.J. Audubon F.R.S.F.L.S.

Lithd Printed & Cold by J.T. Bowen. Phila.

Pl. 343.

Solitary Sandpiper.
1. Male. 2. Female.

Drawn from Nature by J.J. Audubon, F.R.S. F.L.S.

Lith. Printed & Cold by J.T. Bowen, Phila.

Pl. 342.

Spotted Sandpiper
1. Male 2. Female

Drawn from Nature by J.J. Audubon. F.R.S. F.L.S.

Lith. & Printed & Col.d by J.T. Bowen, Phila.

Pl. 345.

Tell-tale Godwit or Snipe.
1. Male. 2. Female.
VIEW OF EAST FLORIDA.

Drawn from Nature By J.J. Audubon, F.R.S.F.L.S

Lith.d Printed & Col.d by J.T.Bowen, Phila.

Pl. 344.

Yellow Shank Snipe.
Male, Summer Plumage.
VIEW IN SOUTH CAROLINA.

Drawn from Nature by J.J.Audubon F.R.S.F.L.S

Lith⁴, Printed & Col⁴ by J.T.Bowen, Phila.

Pl.348.

W.H.

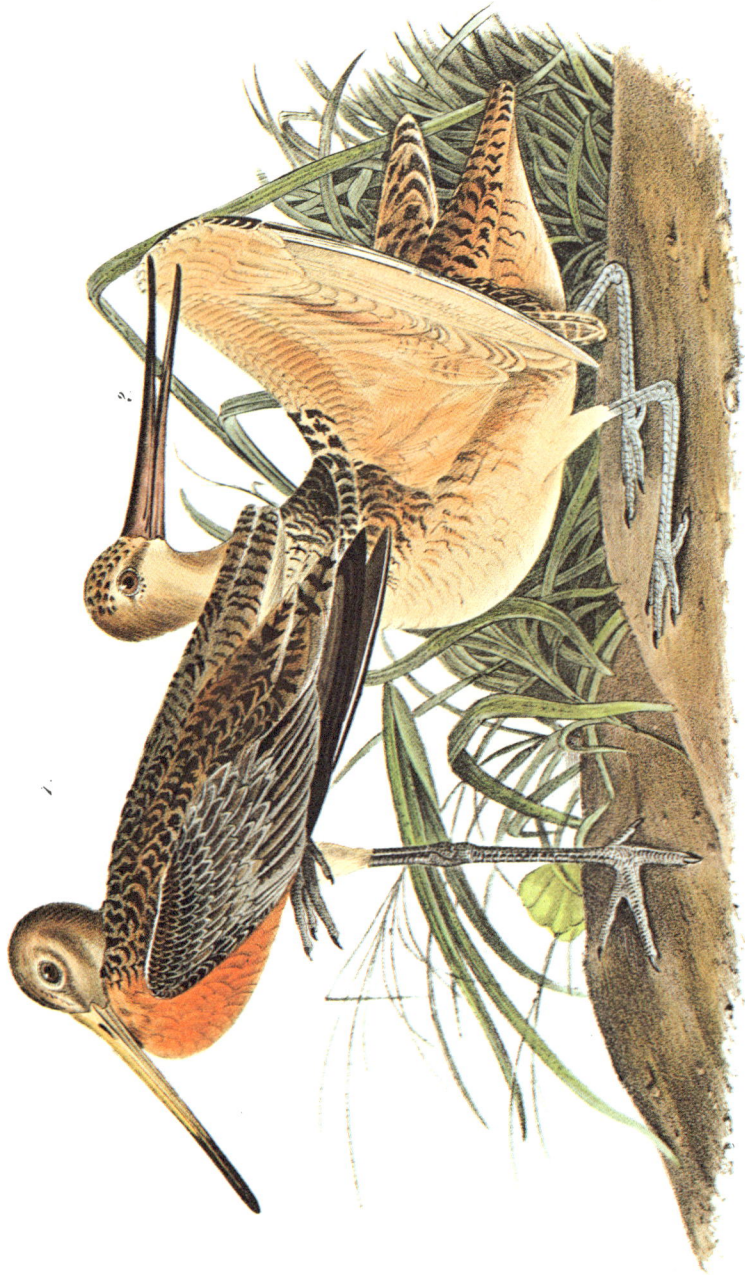

Great Marbled Godwit.

1. Male. 2. Female.

Drawn from Nature by J.J. Audubon, F.R.S.F.L.S.

Lith. & Printed & Col.d by J.T.Bowen, Phila.

Pl. 349.

Hudsonian Godwit.

1. Male. 2. Female Summer Plumage.

Drawn from Nature by J. J. Audubon, F.R.S. F.L.S.

Lith.d Printed & Col.d by J. T. Bowen, Phila.

Pl.351.

Red-breasted Snipe.

1. Spring Plumage. 2. Winter.

Drawn from Nature by J.J. Audubon, F.R.S.F.L.S

Lith. & Printed & Col.d by J.T.Bowen, Phila.

Wilson's Snipe. Common Snipe.
1. Male, 2. & 3 Females.
PLANTATION NEAR CHARLESTON, S.C.

Drawn from Nature by J.J. Audubon. F.R.S.F.L.S.

Lith & Printed & Col⁴ by J.T.Bowen, Phila.

Pl.352.

American Woodcock.

1. Male. 2. Female. 3. Young in Autumn.

Drawn from Nature by J.J. Audubon, F.R.S. F.L.S

Lith & Printed & Col.d by J.T. Bowen, Philad.a

Pl. 353.

American Avocet.

Young in First Winter Plumage. Adult in the Distance.

Drawn from Nature by J. J. Audubon F. R. S. F. L. S.

Lith. d. Printed & Col.d by J. T. Bowen Phila.

Pl. 354.

No. 71.

C. P.

Black Necked Stilt.

Male.

Drawn from Nature by J. J. Audubon, F.R.S. F.L.S.

Lith.d Printed & Cold by J. T. Bowen Phila.

372

Pl. 357.

W.H.

Esquimaux Curlew.
1. Male. 2. Female.

Drawn from Nature by J.J.Audubon.F.R.S.F.L.S.

Lith.&Printed &. Col.d by J.T.Bowen,Phila.

Pl. 356.

Hudsonian Curlew.

Male.

Drawn from Nature by J.J. Audubon, P.R.& L.S.

Lith.d Printed & Col.d by J.T. Bowen, Phila.

Pl. 355.

Long-billed Curlew.
1. Male. 2. Female.
City of Charleston.

Drawn from Nature by J.J.Audubon, F.R.S.F.L.S.

Lith^d Printed & Col^d by J.T.Bowen, Philad^a

Pl.358.

Glossy Ibis
Adult Male.

Drawn from Nature by J.J.Audubon P.R.S.F.L.S

Lith.d Printed & Col.d by J.T.Bowen.Phila.

N°72.

Pl.359.

N°72.
Scarlet Ibis.
1. Adult male 2. Young second Autumn.

Drawn from Nature by J.J. Audubon. F.R.S. F.L.S.

Lith⁴ Printed & Col⁴ by J.T. Bowen, Phila.

White Ibis.

1. Adult, 2. Young in Autumn.

Drawn from Nature by J.J. Audubon, F.R.S. F.L.S.

Lith⁴ Printed & Col⁴ by J.T. Bowen, Phila.

Pl.361.

W.H.

Wood Ibis.

Male

Drawn from Nature by J.J. Audubon F.R.S.F.L.S.   Lithd. Printed & Cold. by J.T. Bowen, Philadª.

Roseate Spoonbill
Male.

Drawn from Nature by J.J.Audubon F.R.S. F.L.S.

Lith⁴ Printed & Col⁴ by J.T.Bowen Philad⁴

Pl. 365.

W.H.

American Bittern

1. Male. 2. Female

Drawn from Nature by J. J. Audubon, F.R.S. F.L.S.

Lith.ª Printed & Col.ª by J. T. Bowen, Phila.

Pl. 363.

N°.73.

Black-Crowned Night Heron, or Qua Bird.
1. Adult. 2. Young.

Drawn from Nature by J. J. Audubon, F.R.S. FL.S.

Lith.d Printed & Col.d by J. T. Bowen, Phila.

382

No. 75.

Pl. 372.

Blue Heron!
1. Male adult Spring Plumage. 2. Young second Year.

Drawn from Nature by J. J. Audubon, F.R.S.F.L.S.

Lith.d Printed & Col.d by J.T. Bowen, Phila.

Great American White Ogret.

1. Male, Spring Plumage. 2. Horned Agama Tapayaxin or Hermandez.

Drawn from Nature by J.J.Audubon. F.R.S.F.L.S.

Irish Printed & Col.d by J.T.Bowen Phila.

Great blue Heron.

Male.

Drawn from Nature by J.J.Audubon,F.R.S.F.L.S.   Lithᵈ Printed & Colᵈ by J.T.Bowen,Philadᵃ

Pl. 308.

Great White Heron.
Male adult, Spring Plumage.

Drawn from Nature by J.J.Audubon, F.R.S. F.L.S.

Lith Printed & Col.d by J.T. Bowen, Philad.a

Green Heron

1. Adult Male. 2. Young in Sept.

Drawn from Nature by J.J.Audubon, F.R.S.F.L.S.

Lith. Printed & Col.d by J.T. Bowen, Phila.

Pl. 366.

No. 74.

W.H.

Least Bittern.

1. Male. 2. Female 3 Young

Drawn from Nature by J.J. Audubon. F.R.S.F.L.S.

Lith.^d Printed & Col.^d by J.T. Bowen. Phila.

Pl. 373.

Louisiana Heron.

Male Adult.

Drawn from Nature by J.J.Audubon,F.R.S.F.L.S.

Lith^d Printed & Col^d by J.T.Bowen, Philad^a

Pl. 371.

No 75.

Reddish Egret

1. Adult, full Spring Plumage. 2. Young in full Spring Plumage two Years old.

Drawn from Nature by J.J. Audubon, F.R.S.F.L.S.   Lith. Printed & Col d by J.T.Bowen, Phila.

C.P.

Snowy Heron
♂ *Male.*

drawn from Nature by J.J. Audubon, F.R.S.F.L.S.

Lith. Printed & Col.d by J.T. Bowen, Phila.

Pl.364.

2

1

C.P.

Yellow Crowned Night Heron

1.Adult Male. Spring Plumage.2.Young in October.

Drawn from Nature by J.J.Audubon, F.R.S.F.L.S.

Lith.d Printed & Col.d by J.T.Bowen, Phila.

Pl.375.

American Flamingo.

Adult Male.

Drawn from Nature by J.J. Audubon F.R.S. F.L.S.

Lith. Printed & Cold by J.T. Bowen Phila.

Pl. 378.

Barnacle Goose.

1. Male. 2. Female.

Drawn from Nature by J. J. Audubon F.R.S.F.L.S.

Lith Printed & Col.d by J.T Bowen, Phila.

Pl.379.

No.76.

W.H.

Brant Goose

1. Male. 2. Female.

Drawn from Nature by J.J. Audubon, F.R.S.F.L.S.

Lith. Printed & Col.d by J.T.Bowen, Philad.a

395

Canada Goose.

1. Male. 2. Female

Drawn from Nature by J.J. Audubon F.R.S.F.L.S

Pl.380.

Drawn from Nature by J.J. Audubon, F.R.S. F.L.S.

W.H.

Lith. Printed & Col.d by J.T. Bowen, Philad.a

White-fronted Goose.
1. Male. 2. Female.

C.P.

Hutchins's Goose.

Adult Male.

Drawn from Nature by J.J. Audubon, F.R.S.FL.S.

Lithd. Printed & Cold. by J.T. Bowen, Philad.

No.77.

Pl.381.

Snow Goose.
1. Adult male. 2. Young Female.

Drawn from Nature by J. J. Audubon, F.R.S. F.L.S.

Lith. Printed & Col.d by J. T. Bowen, Phila.

American Swan.

Male.

Drawn from Nature by J.J. Audubon. F.R.S.F.L.S

Lith Printed & Col.d by J.T. Bowen, Phila

Pl. 382.

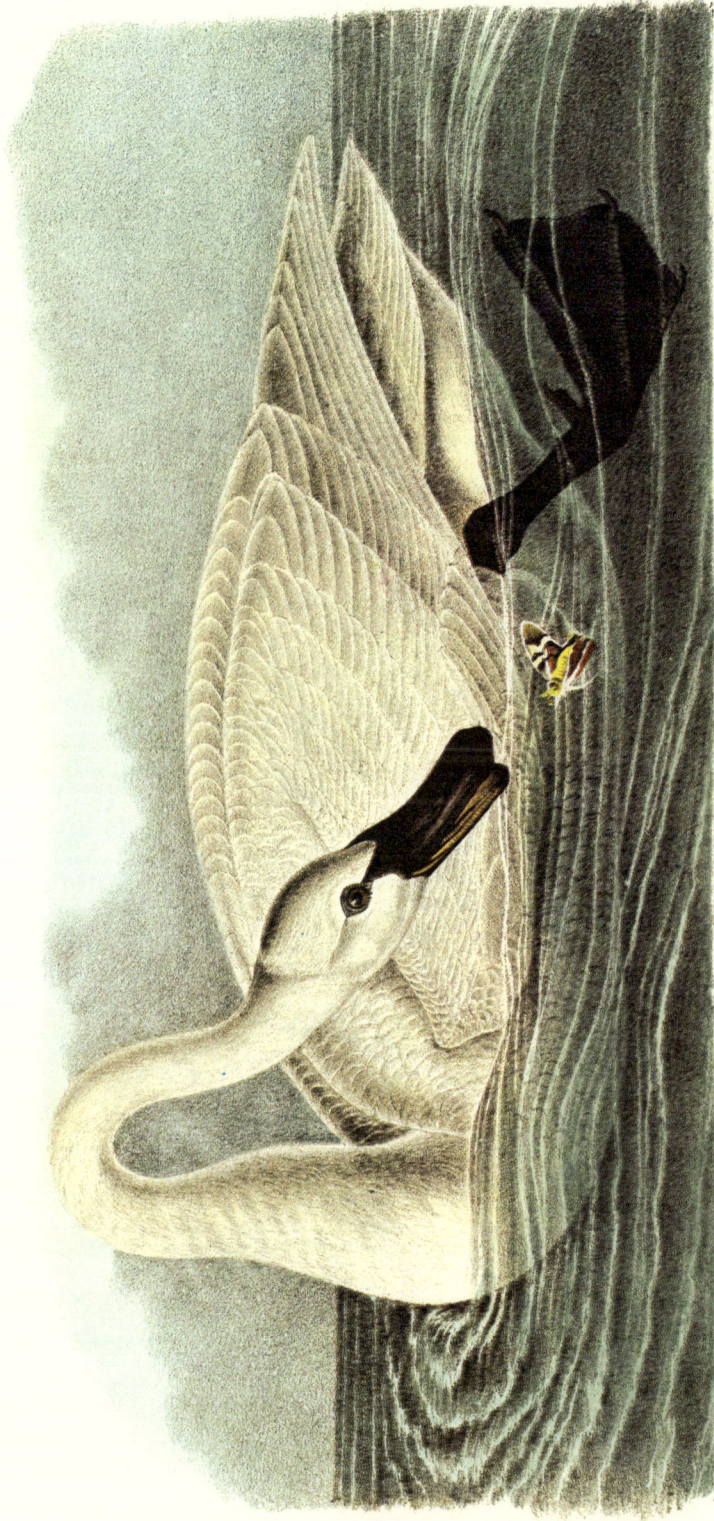

Trumpeter Swan.

Adult.

Drawn from Nature by J.J.Audubon, F.R.S. F.L.S.

Lith. Printed & Col.d by J.T.Bowen, Phila.

Pl. 383.

Trumpeter Swan.
Young.

Drawn from Nature by J. J. Audubon, F.R.S.F.L.S.

Lith. Printed & Col.d by J. T. Bowen, Phila.

Pl.389.

CP. Wild
American Widgeon
1. Male. 2. Female.

Drawn from Nature by J.J.Audubon,F.R.S.F.L.S

Lith Printed & Col.d by J.T.Bowen,Phila

Pl.392.

1.

2.

American Green-winged Teal.
1. Male. 2. Female.

Drawn from Nature by J.J.Audubon, F.R.S. F.L.S.

Lith. Printed & Col.d by J.T.Bowen, Phila.

Pl. 393.

Blue-winged Teale

1. Male. 2. Female.

Drawn from Nature by J.J.Audubon, F.R.S.F.L.S.

Lith.d Printed & Col.d by J. T. Bowen, Philad.a

Pl. 387.

R.T.

Brewer's Duck.

Male

Drawn from Nature by J. J. Audubon. F.R.S. F.L.S.

Lith. Printed & col.ᵈ by J. T. Bowen. Phila.

Pl. 386.

Dusky Duck.
1. Male. 2. Female.

Drawn from Nature by J. J. Audubon, F. R. S. F. L. S.

Lith. Printed & Col.ᵈ by J. T. Bowen, Phila.

Pl.388.

1.

2.

Drawn from Nature by J. J. Audubon, F.R.S. F.L.S.

R. I.
Gadwall Duck.
1. Male. 2. Female.

Lith. Printed & Col.d by J. T. Bowen, Phila.

No.77.

Pl.335.

Mallard

1, 2. Males; 3, 4. Females.

Drawn from Nature by J. J. Audubon, F.R.S.F.L.S.

Lith'd Printed & Col'd by J.T.Bowen, Philad'

Pl. 390

Drawn from Nature by J.J.Audubon, F.R.S.F.L.S.

Pintail Duck.

1. Male. 2. Female.

Lith.d Printed & Col.d by J. T. Bowen, Philad.a

Pl. 394

Shoveller Duck

1 Male. 2 Female.

Drawn from Nature by J.J.Audubon.FRSFLS.

Lith.d Printed & Col.d by J.T.Bowen. Philad.

C.P.

Wood Duck Summer Duck.
1. Male. 2. Female.

Drawn from Nature by J.J. Audubon, F.R.S. F.L.S.

Lith. Printed & Cold by J.T. Bowen, Phila.

Pl. 403.

W.H.

American Scoter Duck.

1. Male. 2. Female.

Drawn from Nature by J.J. Audubon. F.R.S. F.L.S.

Lith. Printed & Col.d by J.T. Bowen, Philad.a

2

Black or Surf Duck.
1. Male. 2. Female.

Drawn from Nature by J.J. Audubon. F.R.S.F.L.S.

Lith. Printed & Cold by J.T. Bowen Philada.

Pl. 108

Buffel-headed Duck

1. Male. 2. Female.

Drawn from Nature by J. J. Audubon. F.R.S.F.L.S.

Lith. Printed & Col.d by J. T. Bowen. Phila.

Pl. 395

Drawn from Nature by J.J.Audubon,F.R.S.F.L.S.

Canvass Back Duck
1 Male 2 Female
VIEW OF BALTIMORE, MARYLAND

Lith⁹ Printed & Col⁹ by J. T. Bowen, Philad⁹

Pl. 498.

Common Scaup Duck.
1. Male. 2. Female.

Drawn from Nature by J.J. Audubon, F.R.S. F.L.S.

Lith. Printed & Col.d by J.T. Bowen, Philad.a

Pl. 405.

Eider Duck.

1. Male. 2. Female.

Drawn from Nature by J. J. Audubon F.R.S.F.L.S.

Lith. Printed & col.d By J.T. Bowen Phila.

418

Pl. 406.

Golden Eye Duck.

1. Male. 2. Female.

Drawn from Nature by J. J. Audubon, F. R. S. F. L. S.

Lith. Printed & Col.d by J. T. Bowen, Philad.a

Harlequin Duck.

1. Old Male. 2. Female. 3. Young Male.

Drawn from Nature by J.J. Audubon, F.R.S.F.L.S.

Lith Printed & Cold by J.T. Bowen, Philada

Pl. 404.

King Duck.
1. Male. 2. Female

Drawn from Nature by J. J. Audubon. F.R.S. F.L.S

Lith Printed & Col.d by J. T. Bowen, Phila

Pl. 410.

Long-tailed Duck.

1. Male, Summer Plumage. 2. Male in Winter. 3. Female and Young.

Drawn from Nature by J. J. Audubon, F.R.S. F.L.S.

Lith Printed & Col.d by J. T. Bowen Philada

Pl. 400.

N°. 80.

Pied Duck.
1. Male 2. Female

Drawn from Nature by J.J. Audubon, F.R.S. F.L.S

Lith Printed & Col.d by J.T.Bowen, Phila.

Pl. 396

Red-headed Duck.

1. Male. 2. Female.

Drawn from Nature by J.J.Audubon, F.R.S.F.L.S.

Lith.ª Printed & Col.ª by J. T. Bowen, Philad.ª

N.º 11.

Pl. 398.

R.T.

Ring-necked Duck

1. Male. 2. Female.

Drawn from Nature by J. J. Audubon, F.R.S. F.L.S.

Lith. Printed & Col.ᵈ by J. T. Bowen, Philad.ᵃ

Pl.399.

W. H.
Ruddy Duck.
1. Male. 2. Female. 3. Young.

Drawn from Nature by J. J. Audubon, F.R.S.F.L.S.

Lith. Printed & Col.d by J. T. Bowen Philad.a

Pl. 397.

R.T.

Scaup Duck.
1. Male. 2. Female.

Drawn from Nature by J.J. Audubon, F.R.S. F.L.S.

Lith Printed & Col.d by J.T. Bowen, Philad.a

Pl. 401.

Velvet Duck.
1. Male. 2. Female.

Drawn from Nature by J.J.Audubon, F.R.S. F.L.S.

Lith Printed & Cold by J.T.Bowen, Phila.

Pl. 407.

Drawn From Nature by J.J. Audubon, F.R.S.P.L.S.

Western Duck,

Males.

Lith. Printed & Col.ª by J.T. Bowen, Philad.ª

Pl. 411.

Buff-breasted Merganser. Goosander.

1. Male. 2. Female.

Drawn from Nature by J.J. Audubon. F.R.S.F.L.S.

Lith. Printed & Col.d by J.T.Bowen, Philad.a

Pl. 443.

N°.83.

Hooded Merganser.
1. Male. 2. Female.

Drawn from Nature by J. J. Audubon. F. R. S. F. L. S.

Lith. Printed & Col.^d by J. T. Bowen Philad.^a

Pl. 412.

Red-breasted Merganser?

1. Male. 2. Female.

Drawn from Nature by J.J. Audubon, F.R.S. F.L.S.

Lith. Printed & Col.d by J.T. Bowen, Philad.a

Pl. 414.

White Merganser. Smew. White Nun

1. Male. 2. Female.

Drawn from Nature by J.J. Audubon, F.R.S. F.L.S.

Lith. Printed & Col. by J.T. Bowen, Philad.

Pl. 415.

Common Cormorant

1. Male. 2. Female 3. Young.

Drawn from Nature by J.J. Audubon, F.R.S.Pl.S.

Lith. Printed & Col.d by J.T.Bowen, Philad.a

Double-crested Cormorant

Male.

Drawn from Nature by J. J. Audubon, P.R.S.F.L.S.   Lith. Printed & Cold by J.T. Bowen, Philada

Pl. 417.

No. 84.

Florida Cormorant
Male

H.W.

Drawn from Nature by J. J. Audubon, F.R.S. P.L.S.

Lith Printed & Col.d by J. T. Bowen, Phila.

436

Pl. 418.

W.H.

Townsend's Cormorant
Male.

Drawn from Nature by J. J. Audubon, F.R.S. F.L.S.   Lith. Printed & Col.ᵈ by J. T. Bowen, Phila

C.P.

Violet green Cormorant

Female in Winter

Drawn from Nature by J.J.Audubon,F.R.S.F.L.S.   Lith.Printed & Colᵈ by J.T.Bowen,Philadᵃ

American Anhinga Snake Bird

1. Male 2. Female

Drawn from Nature by J. J. Audubon F.R.S. F.L.S.   Lith Printed & Col.d by J. T. Bowen Phila.

Frigate Pelican. Man of War Bird.

Drawn from Nature by J. J. Audubon F.R.S.P.L.S.   *Male.*   Lith Printed & Col.d by J.T. Bowen Phila.

W.H.

American White Pelican

Male.

Drawn from Nature by J.J.Audubon, F.R.S.F.L.S.   Lithᵈ Printed & Colᵈ by J. T. Bowen, Philadᵃ

Pl.423.

Brown Pelican.

Adult Male.

Drawn from Nature by J.J Audubon, F.R.S F.L.S

Lith Printed & Col.d by J.T Bowen, Philadelphia

Pl. 424.

N°. 85.

Brown Pelican.
Young first Winter.

Drawn from Nature by J.J. Audubon. F.R.S.F.L.S

Lith Printed & Col.^d by J.T. Bowen, Philad^a

c.p.

Booby Gannet.

Male.

Drawn from Nature by J.J.Audubon, F.R.S.F.L.S

Lith Printed & Cold by J.T.Bowen, Philadᵃ

Common Gannet.

1. Adult male. 2. Young.

Drawn from Nature by J. J. Audubon F.R.S.F.L.S

Lith. Printed & Col.d by J. T. Bowen, Phila.da

Pl. 427.

Tropic Bird

1. Male 2. Female

Drawn from Nature by J. J. Audubon. F.R.S. F.L.S

Lith Printed & Cold by J. T. Bowen, Phila.

Pl. 428.

Black Skimmer or Shearwater.
Male.

Drawn from Nature by J. J. Audubon, F.R.S. F.L.S

Lith Printed & Col.^d by J. T. Bowen, Philad.^a

Arctic Tern.

Male

Drawn from Nature by J. J. Audubon, F.R.S. F.L.S.   Lith Printed & Col.d by J.T. Bowen, Phila.

Black Tern.

1. Adult. 2. Young.

Drawn from Nature by J. J. Audubon, F.R.S.F.L.S.

Lith. Printed & Col.d by J. T. Bowen, Philad.a

Pl. 429.

Cayenne Tern
Male.

Drawn from Nature by J.J.Audubon,F.R.S.F.L.S.

Lith. Printed & Col.d by J.T.Bowen,Philad.a

Pl. 433.

Common Tern

Male. Spring Plumage

Drawn from Nature by J. J. Audubon, F. R. S. F. L. S.

Lith. Printed & Cold by J. T. Bowen, Phila.

Gull billed Tern Marsh Tern.

Male.

Drawn from Nature by J.J.Audubon, F.R.S.F.L.S.   Lith. Printed & Col.d by J.T.Bowen Philad.a

Pl. 434.

Howell's Tern

Adult.

Drawn from Nature by J. J. Audubon F. R. S. F. L. S.

Lith Printed & Col.ᵈ by J. T. Bowen, Philadᵃ.

Least Tern.

1. Adult in Spring 2. Young.

Drawn from Nature by J.J.Audubon, F.R.S.F.L.S.

Lithᵈ Printed & Colᵈ by J. T. Bowen, Philadᵃ

Pl. 440.

Noddy Tern
Male.

Drawn from Nature by J. J. Audubon, F.R.S.F.L.S.

Lith. Printed & Col.d by J. T. Bowen, Philad.a

Pl. 437.

Roseate Tern.

Male

Drawn from Nature by J.J. Audubon, F.R.S.F.L.S

Lith Printed & Col.ª by J.T Bowen, Philadª

Pl. 431.

Sandwich Tern.

Adult

Drawn from Nature by J.J. Audubon, F.R.S. F.L.S

Lith. Printed & Col.d by J.T. Bowen, Phila.

Pl. 432.

Sooty Tern.

Drawn from Nature by J.J. Audubon F.R.S. F.L.S

Lith Printed & Col.ᵈ by J.T Bowen. Phila

Pl. 435.

Trudeau's Tern.

Adult.

Drawn from Nature by J.J.Audubon F.R.S. F.L.S

Lith Printed & Col.d by J.T.Bowen,Phila.

Pl. 443.

Black-headed Gull.

1. Adult Male Spring Plumage. 2. Young First Autumn.

Drawn from Nature by J. J. Audubon, F.R.S. F.L.S.

Lith Printed & Col.d by J. T. Bowen, Phila.

Pl. 442.

N° 89.

Bonapartes Gull.

1. Male in Spring. 2. Female. 3. Young first Autumn.

Pl. 446.

Common American Gull. Ring-billed Gull.
1. Adult 2. Young.

Drawn from Nature by J. J. Audubon, F.R.S. F.L.S.

Pl.441.

Fork-tailed Gull.

Male.

Drawn from Nature by J.J.Audubon.F.R.S.FL.S.

Lith. Printed & Col.d by J.T.Bowen, Philad.a

W.E.H.

Glaucus Gull. Burgomaster

1. Adult male. 2. Young First Autumn.

Drawn from Nature by J.J. Audubon, P.R.S.F.L.S

Lith. Printed & Col.d by J.T. Bowen, Phila.

W.E.H.

Great Black-backed Gull

Male

Drawn from Nature by J. J. Audubon, F.R.S. F.L.S.   Lith Printed & Col.d by J. T. Bowen. Philad.a

W.E.H.

Herring or Silvery Gull
1. Adult in Spring. — 2. Young in Autumn.

Drawn from Nature by J.J.Audubon. F.R.S.F.L.S.   Lith. Printed & Col.d by J. T. Bowen, Philadelphia.

Pl. 445.

Ivory Gull.
1. Adult Male 2. Young second Autumn.

Drawn from Nature by J.J.Audubon, F.R.S. F.L.S.

Lith. Printed & Col.d by J.T.Bowen, Philad.a

Pl.444.

2

1

Kittiwake Gull.
1. Adult. - 2. Young.

Drawn from Nature by J.J.Audubon. F.R.S.F.L.S

Lith. Printed & Col.d by J.T.Bowen, Philad.a

Pl. 447.

No. 90.

White-winged Silvery Gull.
1. Male in Summer. 2. Young in Winter.

Drawn from Nature by J.J.Audubon, F.R.S.F.L.S

Lith. Printed & Col.d by J.T.Bowen, Philadelphia

469

Pl.453.

W.E.H.

Arctic Jager.

Drawn from Nature by J.J. Audubon, F.R.S.F.L.S.

Lith. Printed & Cold by J.T. Bowen, Philad.ª

Pl. 451.

Pomarine Jäger.
Adult Female.

Drawn from Nature by J.J. Audubon, F.R.S.F.L.S.

Lith. Printed & Col.ᵈ by J.T. Bowen, Phila.

Pl. 452.

2.

1.

W.E.H.

Richardson Jager.

1. Male Adult. 2. Young in Novr.

Drawn from Nature by J.J. Audubon, F.R.S. Pl.S.

Lith. Printed & Col.d by J.T. Bowen, Philad.a

Pl. 454.

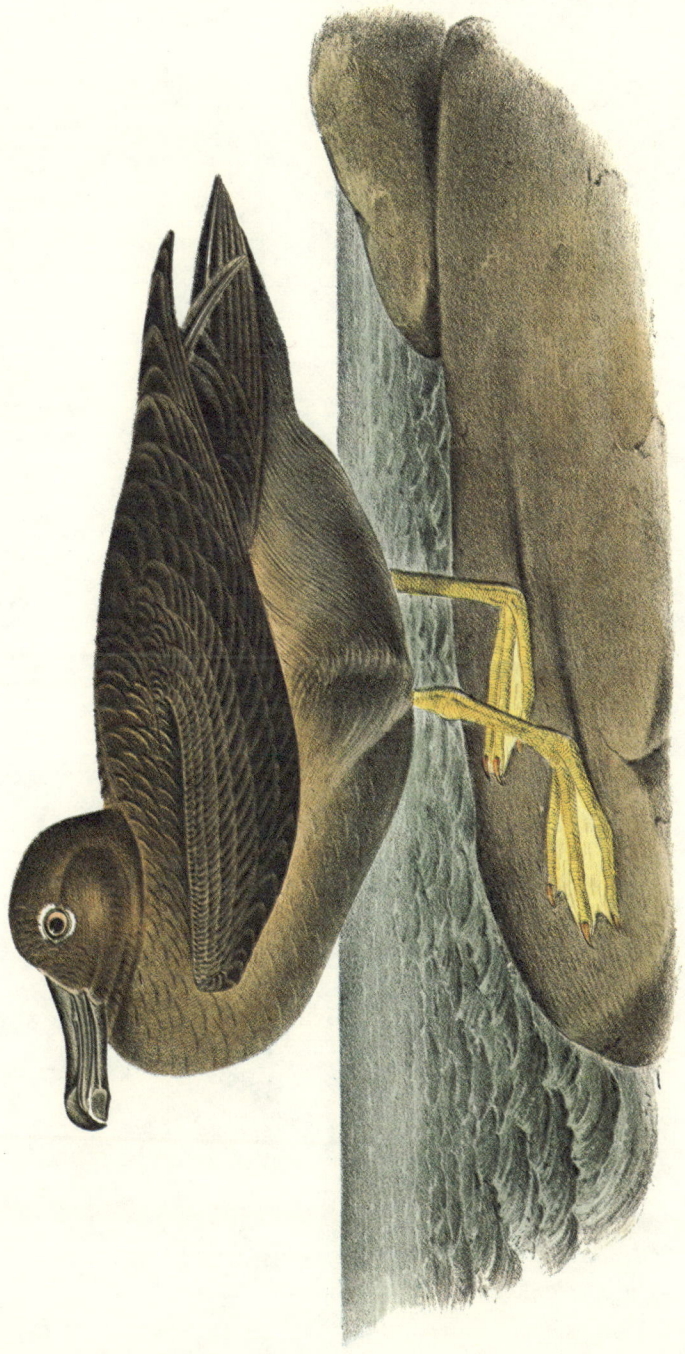

Drawn from Nature by J.J. Audubon F.R.S. F.L.S

Lith. Printed & Col.d by J.T. Bowen, Philad.a

Dusky Albatross

N.º 91.

Fulmar Petrel.

Adult Male Summer Plumage.

W.XII.

Drawn from Nature by J.J.Audubon, F.R.S.F.L.S.

Lith Printed & Cold by J.T.Bowen, Philad.ª

474

Pl.458.

N°.92.

W.E.H.

Dusky Shearwater.
Male in Spring.

Drawn from Nature by J.J.Audubon, F.R.S.F.L.S.

Lith. Printed & Col.ᵈ by J.T.Bowen, Philad.ᵃ

475

Pl. 457.

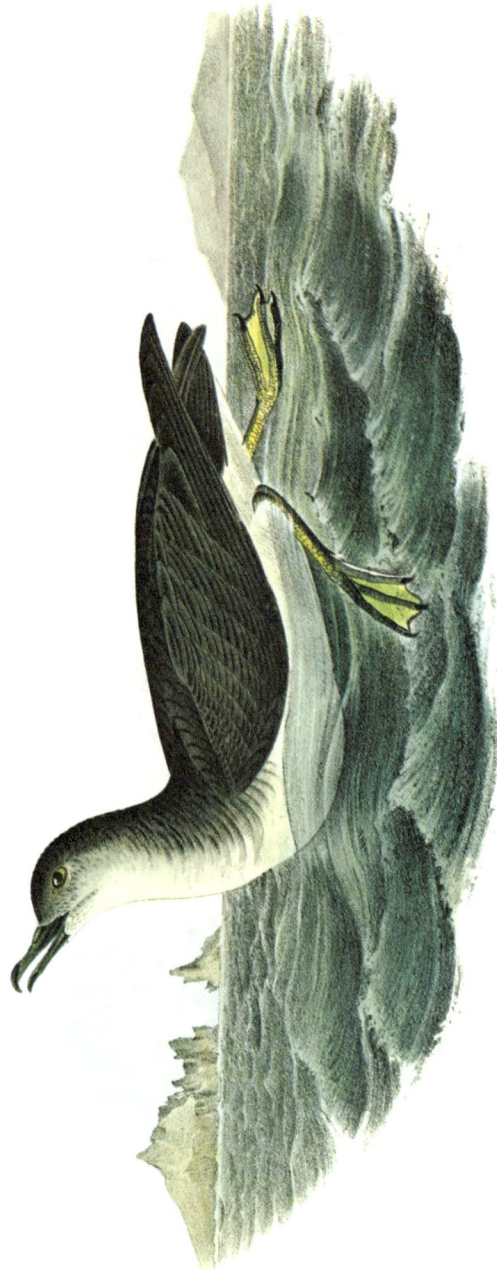

Manks Shearwater

Male

Drawn from Nature by J. J. Audubon, F.R.S. F.L.S

Lith Printed & Col.d by J. T. Bowen, Philada.

Pl. 456.

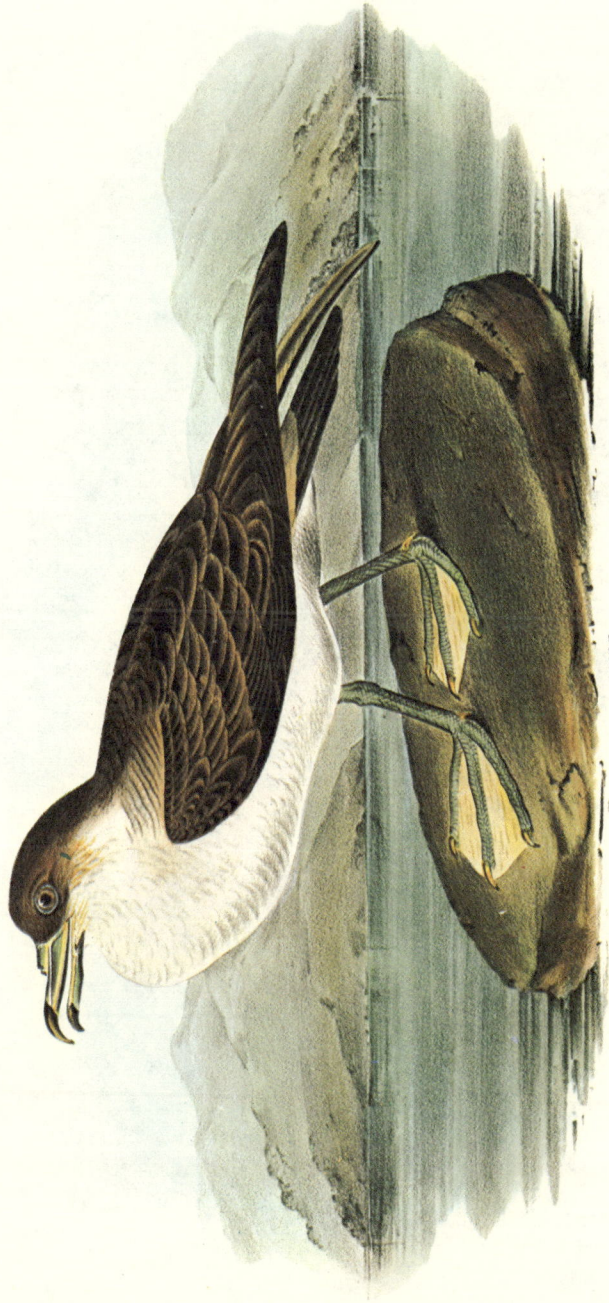

Drawn from Nature by J.J.Audubon, F.R.S.F.L.S.

W.E.H.

Lith. Printed & Col.d by J.T.Bowen, Phila.a

Wandering Shearwater

Male

Pl. 459.

Leach's Petrel. — Forked-tailed Petrel.
1. Male. 2. Female.

Drawn from Nature by J. J. Audubon F.R.S.F.L.S.

Lith. Printed & Col.d by J.T. Bowen Philad.ª

Pl. 461.

Drawn from Nature by J. J. Audubon. F.R.S. &c.

Least Petrel. Mother Carey's chicken?

1. Male. 2. Female.

Lith. Printed & Col.^d by J. T. Bowen, Philadelphia.

Pl. 460.

Wilson's Petrel.— Mother Carey's chicken.
1. Male. 2. Female.

Drawn from Nature by J.J. Audubon, F.R.S. F.L.S

Lith. Printed & Col.d by J.T. Bowen, Philad.a

Pl. 464.

Common or Arctic Puffin.

1. Male. 2. Female.

Drawn from Nature by J. J. Audubon, F.R.S.F.L.S.

Lith. Printed & Col.d by J. T. Bowen, Philad.ª

Pl. 463.

Large billed Puffin.

1. Male 2. Female

Drawn from Nature by J.J. Audubon, F.R.S. F.L.S

Lith Printed & Cold by J.T. Bowen. Philad.ª

Pl. 462.

Tufted Puffin.
1. Male 2. Female.

Drawn from Nature by J.J.Audubon. F.R.S.F.L.S

Lith Printed & Col.d by J.T.Bowen, Philad.a

Pl.465.

Great Auk.
Adult.

Pl. 466.

1.

2.

wt. 11

Razor–billed Auk.)

1. Male. 2. Female.

Drawn from Nature by J.J. Audubon. F.R.S.F.L.S.

Lith Printed & Col.d by J.T. Bowen Philad.a

Pl. 467.

Curled-crested Phaleris

Adult

Drawn from Nature by J. J. Audubon, F.R.S. F.L.S

Lith Printed & Col.d by J. T. Bowen, Philad.a

Pl.468.

Knob-billed Phaleris

Adult.

Drawn from Nature by J.J.Audubon,FRS,FLS

Lith Printed & Col.d by J.T.Bowen, Philad.a

Pl. 469.

Little Auk._Sea dove.

1. Male 2, Female

Drawn from Nature by J. J. Audubon, F.R.S. F.L.S

Lith Printed & Col.d by J.T Bowen Phila

488

Pl. 474.

N°. 95.

Black Guillemot.

Drawn from Nature by J.J.Audubon, F.R.S.F.L.S.

1, Adult.— Summer Plumage. 2, Adult in Winter.— 3, Young.

Lith. Printed & Col.d by J.T.Bowen, Philad.a

Pl. 470.

2.

1.

Black throated Guillemot

1. Adult 2. Young

Drawn from Nature by J.J. Audubon F.R.S. F.L.S.

Pl.473.

W.E.H.

Foolish Guillemot – Murre.
1. Male. 2. Female.

Drawn from Nature by J.J. Audubon, F.R.S. F.L.S.

Lith. Printed & Col.d by J.T. Bowen, Philad.a

Horned-billed Guillemot.

Adult.

Drawn from Nature by J.J.Audubon F.R.S.F.L.S

Lith. Printed & Col.d by J.T.Bowen Philad.a

Pl.472.

Nº95.

Large billed Guillemot.

Male.

Drawn from Nature by J.J.Audubon, F.R.S.F.L.S.

Lith.Printed & Col.ᵈ by J.T.Bowen, Philad.ᵃ

Pl. 475.

N°. 95.

Slender-billed Guillemot.

1. Male. 2. Female.

Drawn from Nature by J.J. Audubon, F.R.S.F.L.S.

Lith. Printed & Col.d by J.T.Bowen, Philad.a

Pl. 477.

N°. 96.

Black-throated Diver

1. Male. 2. Female. 3. Young in Octr.

Drawn from Nature by J.J. Audubon, F.R.S. F.L.S.

Lith. Printed & Col.d by J.T. Bowen, Phila.

Pl. 476.

Great North Diver. Loon.

1. Adult. 2. Young in Winter.

Drawn from Nature by J. Audubon F.R.S. F.L.S.

Lith. Printed & Cold. by J.T. Bowen Philad.ª

Pl. 478.

W.E.H.

Red-throated Diver.

1. Male Summer Plumage. 2. do Winter 3. Female 4. Young

Drawn from Nature by J.J.Audubon, P.R.S.F.L.S

Lith. Printed & Col.d by J.T.Bowen, Philad.a

Pl.479.

Crested Grebe.

1. Adult Male in Spring. 2. Young (First Winter)

Drawn from Nature by J. J. Audubon, F. R. S. F. L. S.

Lith Printed & Col. d by J.T. Bowen, Phila.

Pl. 482.

Eared Grebe.

1 Male. 2 Young. First Year.

Drawn from Nature by J. J. Audubon, F.R.S. F.L.S.

Lith. Printed & Cold. by J. T. Bowen, Philad.ª

Pl. 481.

W.E.H.

Horned Grebe.

1. Adult Male. 2. Female in Winter.

Drawn from Nature by J.J.Audubon, F.R.S.F.L.S.

Lith. Printed & Col.d by J.T.Bowen, Philad.a

Pl. 483.

Pied-billed Dobchick.

1. Male, 2. Female.

Drawn from Nature by J. J. Audubon, F.R.S.F.L.S.

Lith Printed & Col.d by J. T. Bowen Philad.a

Pl. 480.

Red-necked Grebe.

1. Adult Male Spring Plumage 2 Young Winter Plumage

Drawn from Nature by J. J. Audubon, F.R.S. F.L.S.

Lith Printed & Col.d by J.T. Bowen, Philad.a

BOOK OF
MAMMALS

Plate LXXVII

Drawn from Nature by J. W. Audubon

On Stone by W.ᵐ E. Hitchcock

Lith. Printed & Col.ᵈ by J. T. Bowen, Phil.

Prong-Horned Antelope.

Plate CXXIII.

Nº 25.

On Stone by W.E.Hitchcock.

Drawn from Nature by J.W.Audubon.

Lith.ᵈ Printed & Col.ᵈ by J.T.Bowen.,Philad.ᵃ

The Sewellel.

Plate CIII

N°. 21

Drawn from nature by J.W. Audubon.

Hoary Marmot. The Whistler.

Lith. Printed & Col.d by J.T. Bowen, Phil.

Plate CVII

Drawn from Nature by J.W. Audubon

Drawn on Stone by Wm E. Hitchcock

Lith. Printed & Col.d by J.T. Bowen, Phil.

Louis' Marmot.

Plate II

Nº 1.

Drawn on Stone by R. Trembly

Drawn from Nature by J. Audubon F.R.S. F.L.S.

Maryland. Marmot. Woodchuck. Groundhog.
Old & Young.

Printed by Nagel & Weingærtner. N.Y.

Plate CXXXIV.

Drawn from Nature by J. W. Audubon.

On stone by W. E. Hitchcock.

Lith. Printed & Col. by J. T. Bowen Philad.ᵃ

Yellow-bellied Marmot.

Plate LXXX

Drawn from Nature by J. Audubon, FRS.FLS

Lith. Printed & Col.d by J.T. Bowen, Phil.

Leconte's Pine Mouse.

Plate CXIX

On Stone by W E Hitchcock

Lith. Printed & Col.d by J T Bower, Phil.

Drawn from Nature by J W Audubon.

Northern Meadow Mouse

Plate CXLVII

Fig 1

Fig.2.

Fig.3

On Stone by Wᵐ E Hitchcock.

Fig.1 *American Souslik.* Fig.2 *Oregon Meadow Mouse.* Fig.3 *Texan Meadow Mouse.*

Drawn from Nature by J.W. Audubon

Lith. Printed & Colᵈ by J.T.Bowen, Phil

Plate CXXXV.

N°. 27.

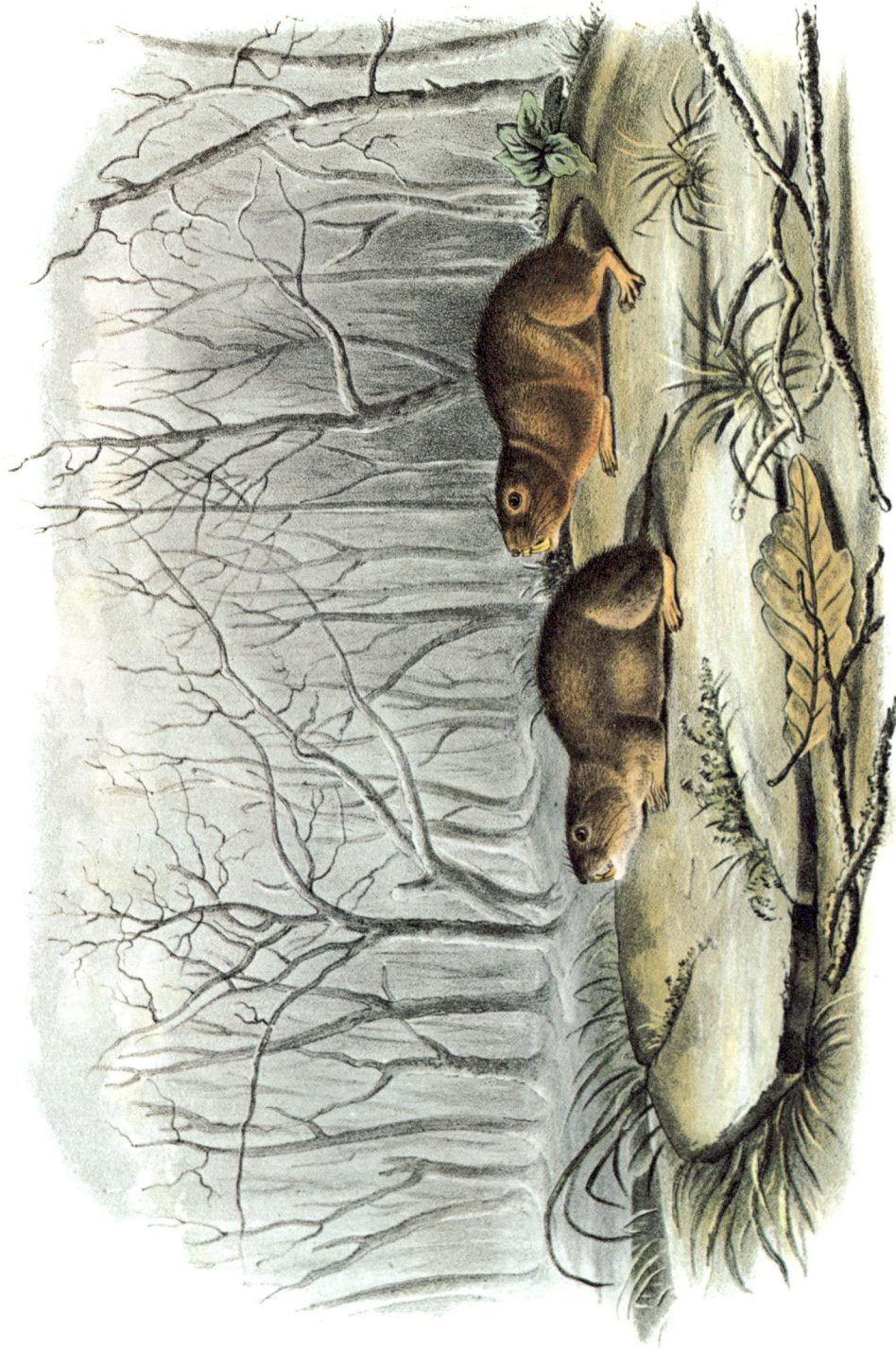

Drawn from Nature by J.W.Audubon.

On stone by W.E.Hitchcock

Lith.d Printed & Col.d by J.T.Bowen, Philad.

Richardson's Meadow Mouse.

514

Plate CXLIV

Fig. 1.

Fig 2   On Stone by Wm E. Hitchcock

Fig 3

Fig 1. Townsends Arvicola.   Fig 2. Sharp-nosed Arvicola.   Fig 3. Bank Rat

Drawn from Nature by J.W. Audubon

Lith Printed & Col.^d by J.T. Bowen, Phil

Plate XLV

Drawn from Nature by J.J.Audubon. F.R.S. F.L.S.

Wilson's Meadow Mouse.

Lith. Printed & Col.d by J.T.Bowen, Philada.

Plate CXV.

On Stone by W.E. Hitchcock

Lith⁴ Printed & Col⁴ by J.T. Bowen, Philadª.

Drawn from Nature by J.W. Audubon.

Yellow-cheeked Meadow Mouse.

On Stone by Wᵐ E. Hitchcock.

Ring-Tailed Bassaris.

Drawn from Nature by J W Audubon   Lith Printed & Colᵈ by J T Bowen, Phiᵃ

Plate LVI

On Stone by Wm F. Hitchcock

Drawn from Nature by J. J. Audubon. F.R.S. F.L.S

Lith. Printed & Col^d by J. Bowen, Phil.

American Bison or Buffalo

No. 12

Plate LVII

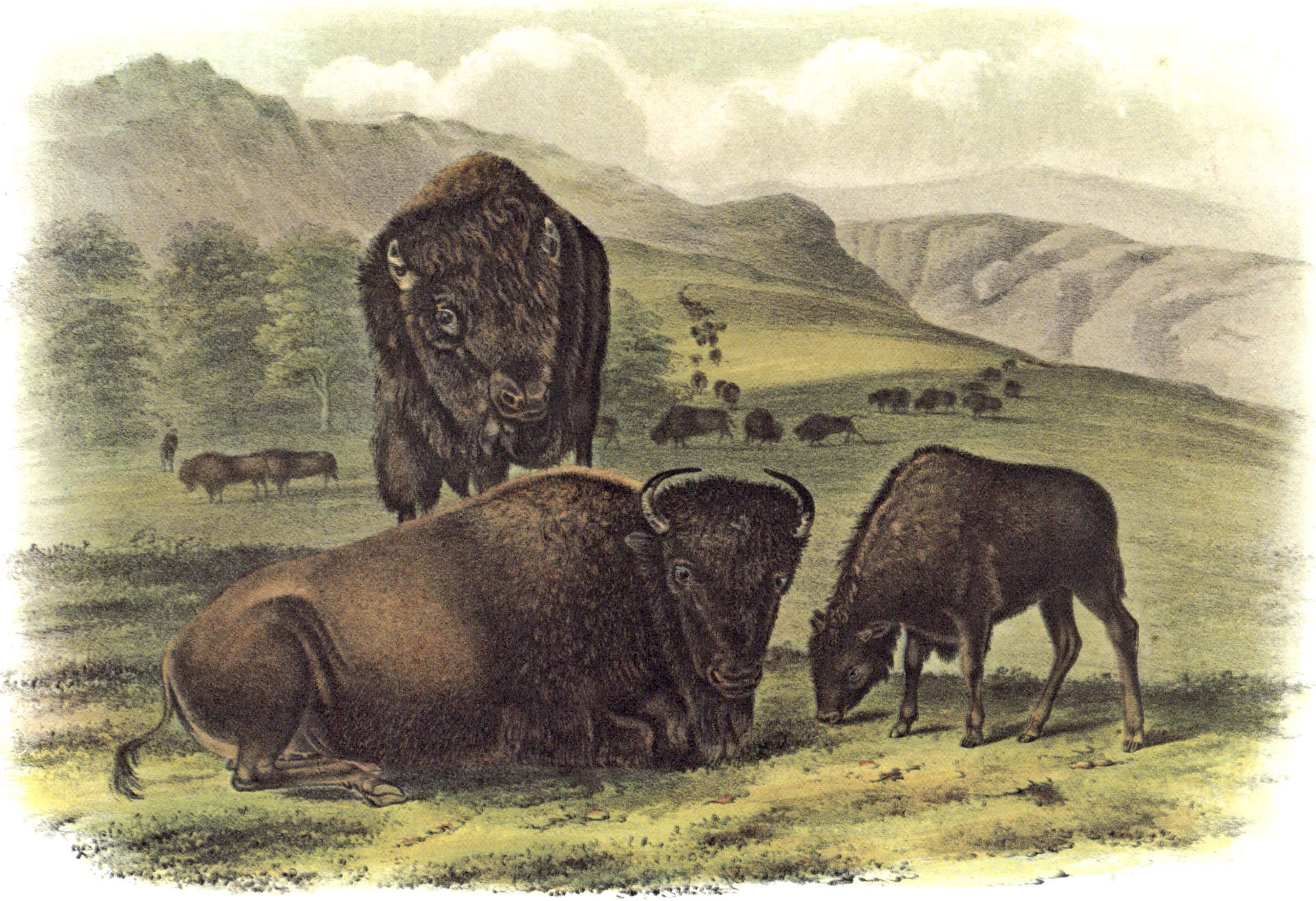

On Stone by Wm. E. Hitchcock

Drawn from Nature by J.J. Audubon, F.R.S.F.L.S

American Bison or Buffalo

Printed & Col.d by J.T. Bowen, Philada.

Plate LXVII

On Stone by W.E. Hitchcock

Drawn from Nature by J. W. Audubon

Lith. Printed & Col.d by J. T. Bowen, Phil.

Black American Wolf

Plate CXIII.

Drawn from Nature by J.W. Audubon

Drawn on Stone by Wm E. Hitchcock

Esquimaux Dog.

Lith Printed & Col^d by J.T.Bowen, Phil

Plate CXXXII

On stone by W.E.Hitchcock.

Hare-Indian Dog.

Lith Printed & Col⁴ by J.T.Bowen, Philad⁴

Drawn from Nature by J.W Audubon

Plate LXXI

No.15.

On Stone by Wm. E. Hitchcock

Drawn from Nature by J W Audubon

Lith. Printed & Cold by J.T. Bowen, Philad

Prairie Wolf.

Plate LXXXII.

Drawn from Nature by J.W. Audubon.

On stone by W.E. Hitchcock

Lith⁴ Printed & Col⁴ by J.T. Bowen, Philad⁴

Red Texan Wolf.

Plate LXXII

N°.15

On. Stone by Wm E. Hitchcock

White American Wolf

Drawn from Nature by J. W. Audubon

Lith. Printed & Col^d by J.T. Bowen, P:.:

Plate CXXVIII

No 26

Drawn from Nature by J.W. Audubon.

On Stone by Wm E. Hitchcock

Lith Printed & Col'd by J.T Bowen: Phil.

Rocky Mountain Goat.

Plate XLV.

On Stone by W E Hitchcock

Drawn from Nature by J.J. Audubon, F.R.S.F.L.S

Lith Printed & Col.d by J.T Bowen, Philada

American Beaver

Plate LXXVII

On Stone by Wm E. Hitchcock

Lith. Printed & Col^d by J.T. Bowen, Phil

Black-tailed Deer

Drawn from Nature by J.W. Audubon

Plate CVI.

Drawn from Nature by J.W. Audubon.

On Stone by W.E. Hitchcock.

Lith Printed & Col⁴ by J.T. Bowen, Philad⁴

Columbian Black-Tailed Deer.

Plate LXXXI

Drawn from Nature by J.W. Audubon

On Stone by Wm E. Hitchcock

Lith. Printed & Col.^d by J.T. Bowen Phil.

Common American Deer.

Plate CXXXVI

N° 28

On Stone by Wᵐ E. Hitchcock.

Drawn from Nature by J.W. Audubon.

Lith Printed & Colᵈ by J.T.Bowen,Phil

Common or Virginian Deer.

Plate CXVIII

N°. 24.

On Stone by W.E.Hitchcock.

Lith.d Printed & Col.d by J.T.Bowen, Philad.ª

Long-tailed Deer.

Drawn from Nature by J.W.Audubon.

Plate LXXVI

On Stone by W. E. Hitchcock

Lith⁴ Printed & Col⁴ by J.T.Bowen, Philad⁴.

Drawn from Nature by J W.Audubon.

Moose Deer

Plate LXIX

On Stone by W. E. Hitchcock

Drawn from Nature by J. J. Audubon F.R.S.F.L.S.

Common Star-Nose Mole.

Plate CXLVI

Drawn from Nature by J.W Audubon

On Stone by Wᵐ E. Hitchcock

Lith. Printed & Colᵈ by J.T. Bowen, Phil

Nine-banded Armadillo

Plate LXVI

On Stone by Wᵐ. E. Hitchcock

Virginian Opossum.

Drawn from Nature by J.J. Audubon, F.R.S.F.L.S

Lith Printed & Colᵈ by Wᵐ Bowen Philᵃ

Drawn from Nature by J W Audubon

On Stone by Wm. E. Hitchcock

Lith Printed & Col.d by J T Bowen, Phil.

Pouched Jerboa Mouse

538

Plate XXXI

No 7

Drawn on Stone by R Trembly.

Collared Peccary.

Printed by Nagel & Weingærtner N.Y.

Drawn from Nature by J.J.Audubon F.R.S.F.L.S.

539

Plate LXII

Drawn from Nature by J.J. Audubon, F.R.S.F.L.S.

On Stone by W.E. Hitchcock

Lith. Printed & Col⁴ by J.T. Bowen, Phil.

American Elk.- Wapiti Deer.

Plate CXXXVII.

N°28.

Drawn from Nature by J W Audubon.

Lith. Printed & Col^d by J T Bowen, Philad^a.

Sea Otter

The Cougar.

Female & Young.

Plate XCVI

Lith. Printed & Col.d by J.T. Bowen, Phil.a

Drawn on Stone by Wm E. Hitchcock.

The Cougar.
Male.

Drawn from Nature by J. W. Audubon

Plate CI

Drawn from Nature by J. W. Audubon.

On Stone by W. E. Hitchcock.

Lith. Printed & Col.d by J. T. Bowen. Phila.d

The Jaguar.

Plate LXXXVI

On Stone by W.ᵐ E. Hitchcock

Lith. Printed & Col.ᵈ by J T Bowen, Phil.

Drawn from Nature by J W Audubon

Ocelot or Leopard-Cat.

Plate XIII

Drawn on Stone by W^m. E. Hitchcock

Lith. Printed & Col^d by J.T. Bowen, Phil

Drawn from Nature by J.J.Audubon,F.R.S.F.L.S

Mush. Rat.— Musquash.

Old & Young.

Plate CIX

Drawn on Stone by Wm E Hitchcock

Lith Printed & Cold by JT Bowen, Phil

Drawn from Nature by J.W. Audubon

Hudson's Bay Lemming

Plate CXX

Drawn from Nature by J.W. Audubon

Drawn on Stone by Wm E. Hitchcock

Lith. Printed & Col^d by JT. Bowen, Phil

Fig. 1   Tawny Lemming.   Figs 2 & 3   Back's Lemming.

Plate XXVI.

Nº 6.

Drawn on stone by R. Trembly

Wolverine.

Printed & Colᵈ by J.T.Bowen, Philadᵃ

Drawn from Nature by J.J.Audubon,F.R.S.F.L.S.

549

Canada Porcupine.

Drawn from Nature by J.J.Audubon. FRS FLS.

Lith^d. Printed & Col^d by J.T. Bowen, Philad^a

Plate LXXXIII

Drawn from Nature by J.J.Audubon, F.R.S.P.L.S.

On Stone by Wᵐ E. Hitchcock

Lith. Printed & Colᵈ by J.T.Bowen, Phil

Little Chief Hare.

Plate CVIII

On Stone by W.B.Hitchcock

Lith.ª Printed & Col.ª by J.T.Bowen Philad.ª

Bachman's Hare

Drawn from Nature by J.W.Audubon

Plate LXIII

On Stone by W. E. Hitchcock

Black-tailed Hare.

Drawn from Nature by J. J. Audubon, F.R.S. F.L.S

Lith Printed & Col.ᵈ by J.T. Bowen, Philad.ᵃ

Plate CXII.

Drawn on stone by W.E.Hitchcock.

Lith.Printed&Col.d by J.T.Bowen, Philad.a

Californian Hare.

Drawn from Nature by J.W.Audubon.

Plate XXII

Nº 5

Drawn on Stone by R. Trembly.

Grey Rabbit.
Old & Young.

Drawn from Nature by J J Audubon. F.R.S., F.L.S.

Printed by Nagel & Weingærtner. N.Y.

Plate XVIII

Drawn on Stone by R Trembly

Marsh Hare.

Drawn from Nature by J.J Audubon. F.R.S. F.L.S.

Printed by Nagel & Weingærtner N.Y.

Plate XI

No.3.

Drawn from Nature by J.J.Audubon. F.R.S.F.L.S.

Drawn on Stone by R. Trembly.

Northern Hare - (Old & Young)

Summer pelage.

Printed by Nagel & Weingærtner.N.Y

Plate XII

N°.3.

Northern Hare

Winter pélage.

Drawn from Nature by J.J.Audubon, F.R.S.F.L.S.

Drawn on Stone by R.Trembly.

Printed by Nagel & Weingärtner N.Y.

Colored by J.Lawrence

Plate XCIV

Drawn from Nature by J.W.Audubon

On Stone by Wm E.Hitchcock

Lith Printed & Col^d by J T.Bowen, Phil

Nuttall's Hare.

559

Plate XXXII.

Drawn on stone by R. Trembly

Polar Hare

Printed & Col.d by J.T.Bowen, Philad.a

Drawn from Nature by J.J.Audubon, F.R.S.F.L.S.

Plate XXXVII.

N° 8.

Drawn on Stone by R. Trembly

Drawn from Nature by J J Audubon, F.R.S. F.L.S.

Lith Printed & Col⁴ by J T Bowen, Phil

Swamp Hare

Male.

Plate CXXXIII.

Drawn from Nature by J.W. Audubon

On stone by W.E. Hitchcock

Texian Hare.

Lith. Printed & Col.ᵈ by J.T. Bowen. Philad.ᵃ

Plate III.

No. I.

Drawn on Stone by R. Trembly

Drawn from Nature by J.J. Audubon F.R.S, F.L.S.

Townsend's Rocky Mountain Hare
Male & Female

Printed by Nagel & Wemgærtner N.Y.

Plate LXXXVIII.

No 18

On Stone by W E Hitchcock.

Worm-wood Hare.

Drawn from Nature by J.J.Audubon, F.R.S.F.L.S.

Lith.d Printed & Col.d by J.T.Bowen, Philad.a

564

Plate LI

Drawn from Nature by J. Audubon F.R.S.F.L.S.

Lith. Printed & Co. by J.T. Bowen, Philad.ᵃ

Canada Otter.

Plate CXXII

On Stone by W^mE Hitchcock

Canada Otter

Drawn from Nature by J.W.Audubon

Plate XVI

Drawn on Stone by R. Trembly

Printed by Nagel & Weingærtner N.Y.

Canada Lynx.
Male

Drawn from Nature by J.J Audubon F.R.S.F.L.S.

Plate I.

Nº1.

Drawn from Nature by J.J.Audubon. F.R.S. F.L.S.

Drawn on Stone by R.Trembly

Common American Wild-cat.
Male.

Printed by Nagel & Weingærtner N.Y.

568

Plate XCII

On Stone by Wᵐ E Hitchcock

Texan Lynx

Lith Printed & Colᵈby JTBowen, Phil

Drawn from Nature by J W Audubon

Plate XLVII

Drawn from Nature by J.J. Audubon, F.R.S.F.L.S

American Badger

Lith. Printed & Colᵈ by J.T. Bowen, Philada

Common American Skunk.

Drawn from Nature by J.J.Audubon.F.R.S.F.L.S.   Lith Printed & Col.ᵈ by J.T.Bowen. Philadᵃ

On Stone by W.E.Hitchcock.

Large-Tailed Skunk.

Drawn from Nature by J.W.Audubon.   Lith Printed & Col by J.T.Bowen, Philad.

Plate LIII

Drawn from Nature by J.J. Audubon, F.R.S.F.L.S.

On Stone by W^m E Hitchcock

Lith. Printed & Col^d by J.T. Bowen, Phil.

Texan Skunk.

Plate LXXV

Drawn from Nature by J. J. Audubon. F.R.S.F.L.S.

On Stone by Wm E. Hitchcock

Lith Printed & Col^d by J. T. Bowen, Phil^a.

Jumping Mouse.

Plate XL

N.° 8

Drawn on Stone by Wm E. Hitchcock.

Drawn from Nature by J.J.Audubon.P.R.S. F.L.S.

Lith. Printed & Col.^d by J.T.Bowen, Philad.^a

White Footed Mouse.

Plate XXIII

Drawn on Stone by R Trembly.

Black Rat

Old & Young.

Printed by Nagel & Weingartner, N.Y.

Drawn from Nature by J.J.Audubon. F.R.S.F.L.S.

Plate LIV

On Stone by Wm E. Hitchcock

Lith. Printed & Col.d by J.T. Bowen, Phil.

Brown or Norway Rat

Drawn from Nature by J. Audubon, F.R.S.F.L.S

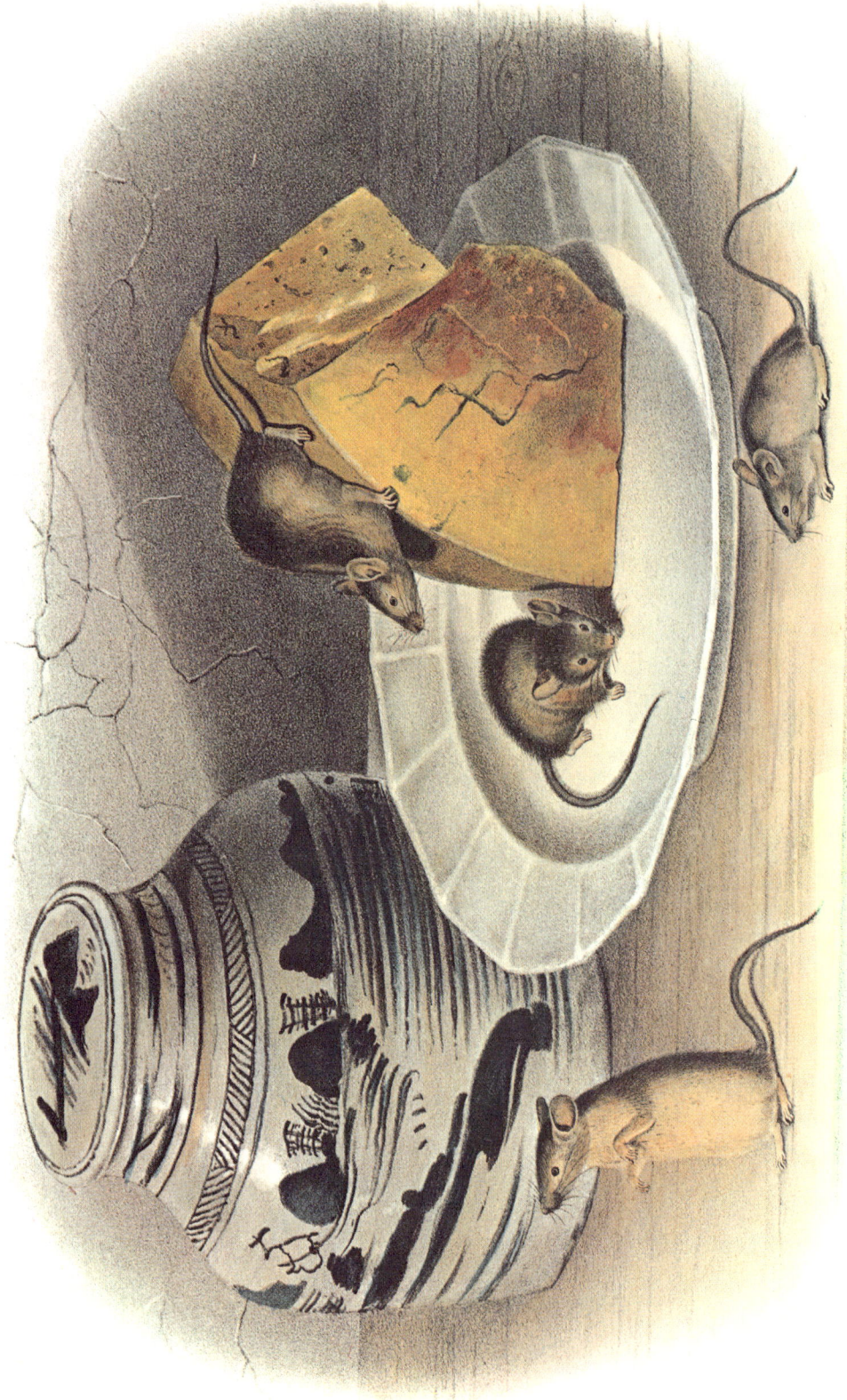

Plate XC

On Stone by Wm E Hitchcock

On. Printed & Col⁴ by J.T. Bowen, Phil.

Common Mouse.

Drawn from Nature by J.W. Audubon.

Nº 18

578

Plate LXV.

N.º 13

Drawn from Nature by J. J. Audubon, F.R.S.L.S.

On Stone by W. E. Hitchcock.

Little Harvest Mouse.

Plate C.

On Stone by W.E.Hitchcock.

Drawn from Nature by J.W.Audubon.

Lith.Printed & Col.by J.T.Bowen,Philad.ª

Missouri Mouse.

Plate XCV

Drawn from Nature by J W Audubon.

On Stone by Wᵐ E Hitchcock

Lith Printed & Colᵈ by J.T Bowen, Phil

Orange Colored Mouse

Drawn on Stone by W.E. Hitchcock

Pennant's Marten or Fisher.

Drawn from Nature by J.J. Audubon, FRS FLS   Lith.ᵈ Printed & Col.ᵈ by J.T.Bowen. Philadᵃ

Plate CXXXVIII

Drawn from Nature by J W Audubon

On Stone by W E Hitchcock

Lith. Printed & Col'd by J T Bowen, Phil.

Pennant's Marten

Plate IV

Drawn on Stone by Wᵐ E. Hitchcock

Florida Rat.

Male, Female & Young of different ages

Drawn from Nature by J.J.Audubon, F.R.S.FL.S

Lith Printed & Colᵈ by J.T.Bowen, Phil

584

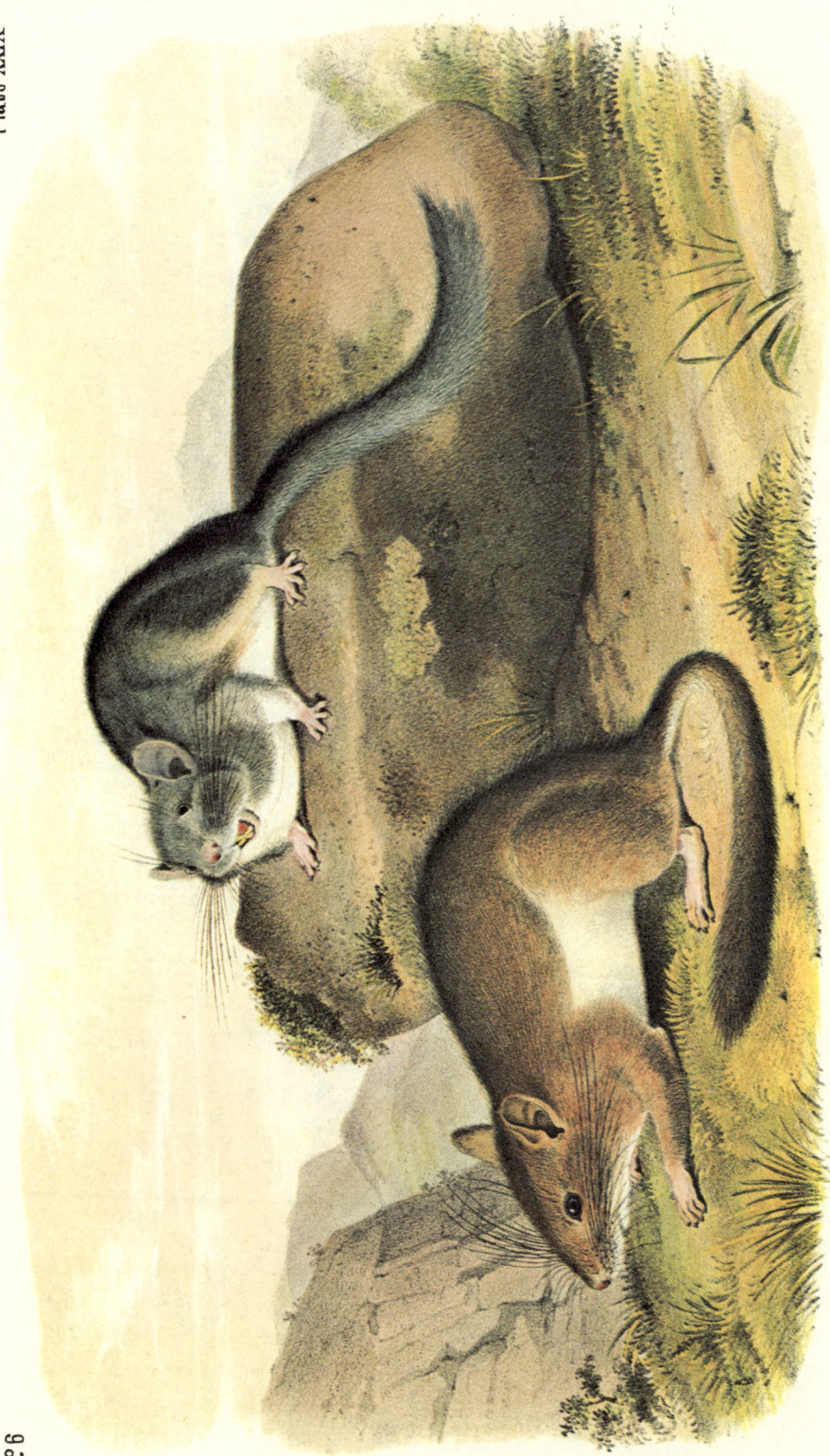

Plate XXIX

No. 6

Drawn on Stone by R. Trembly

Rocky Mountain Neotoma

Drawn from Nature by J.J Audubon. F.R.S.F.L.S.

Printed by Nagel &Weingærtner N.Y

Plate CXI.

Drawn from Nature by J.W.Audubon.

Drawn on Stone by Wm. E. Hitchcock

Lith Printed & Cold by J.T. Bowen. Phil

Musk Ox.

586

Plate LXXIII

Drawn from Nature by J. W. Audubon

On Stone by Wᵐ E. Hitchcock

Lith. Printed & Col.ᵈ by J.T. Bowen, Phil.

Rocky Mountain Sheep.

Plate CLV

On Stone by Wᵐ E. Hitchcock.

Lith. Printed & Col.ᵈ by J.T. Bowen, Phil.

Crab : eating Racoon.

Drawn from Nature by J W Audubon

Plate LXI

On Stone by W. H. Hitchcock

Raccoon.

Drawn from Nature by J. W. Audubon

Lith. Printed & Col.ᵈ by J.T. Bowen, Phil

Plate CXLII.

Drawn from Nature by J. W. Audubon

On Stone by Wm B. Hitchcock

The Camas Rat

Lith. Printed & Col.d by J. T. Bowen, Phil.

Plate XLIV

Drawn from Nature by J. J. Audubon, F.R.S. F.L.S.

Canada Pouched Rat.

Lith Printed & Col⁴ by J.T. Bowen, Philad⁴.

591

Plate CV.

Drawn from Nature by J.W. Audubon.

On Stone by W.E. Hitchcock

Lith.d Printed & Col.d by J.T. Bowen, Philad.a

Columbia Pouched Rat.

Plate CX.

On Stone by W.E.Hitchcock.

Lith⁴ Printed & Col⁴ by J.T.Bowen.Philad⁴.

Mole-shaped Pouched Rat.

Drawn from Nature by J.W.Audubon.

Plate CL.

Fig 1. *Southern Pouched Rat.* Fig 2. *Dekay's Shrew.* Fig 3. *Long-Nosed Shrew.* Fig 4. *Silvery Shrew Mole.*

Drawn from Nature by J.W.Audubon.

On Stone by Wm.E Hitchcock

Lith.Printed & Col.d by J.T.Bowen,Phil

Drawn on Stone by R. Trembly

Common Flying Squirrel
1,2 Males, 3,4 Females, 5 Young

Drawn from Nature by J.J.Audubon F.R.S. F.L.S.

Printed by Nagel & Weingærtner N Y

Drawn on Stone by Wᵐ E. Hitchcock

Oregon Flying Squirrel.

Drawn from Nature by J.J.Audubon,F.R.S.F.L.S.   Lith Printed & Colᵈ by J.T.Bowen,Phil

Plate CXLIII

Fig 1 Severn River Flying Squirrel

Fig 2 Rocky Mountain Flying Squirrel

Plate XCIII

Drawn from Nature by J.W. Audubon.

On Stone by W.E. Hitchcock.

Lith. Printed & Col'd by J.T. Bowen. Phil.

Black Footed Ferret

Plate LX

Drawn from Nature by J.J.Audubon, F.R.S.F.L.S.

On Stone by Wm E. Hitchcock

Lith. Printed & Col^d by J.T. Bowen, Phil^a

Bridled Weasel.

Plate LXIV

On Stone by W.H.Hitchcock

Little American Brown Weasel.

Lith Printed & Colᵈ by J.T Bowen, Phil.

Drawn from Nature by J.W Audubon.

Plate CXL.

No. 28.

Drawn from Nature by J.W.Audubon.

On stone by W.E.Hitchcock

Lith.ᵈ Printed & Col.ᵈ by J.T. Bowen Philad.ᵃ

Little Nimble Weasel.

Plate XXXIII.

Drawn on stone by R. Trembly

Printed & Col.^d by J.T Bowen, Philad.^a

Mink.

Male & Female

Drawn from Nature by J.J.Audubon.F.R.S F.L.S.

Plate CXXIV

N° 25

On Stone by Wᵐ E. Hitchcock

Drawn from Nature by J.W. Audubon

Lith. Printed & Col. by J.T. Bowen, Phil.

Mountain Brook Mink.

Plate CXLVIII

Drawn from Nature by J.W. Audubon

On Stone by Wm E. Hitchcock

Tawny Weasel.

Lith. Printed & Col^d by J.T. Bowen, Phil.

604

Plate LIX.

White Weasel; Stoat.

Drawn from Nature by J.J. Audubon F.R.S.F.L.S.

Lith⁴ Printed & Col⁴ by J.T. Bowen, Philad⁴

Plate CXXVI

On Stone by Wᵐ E. Hitchcock

Drawn from Nature by J.W. Audubon.

Lith. Printed & Colᵈ by J.T Bowen, Phil.

Caribou or American Rein-Deer.

Plate LXXIV

N° 15

On Stone by W. E. Hitchcock

Drawn from Nature by J. Audubon, FRS FLS

Lith Printed & Col d by J.T. Bowen, Phil

Brewer's Shrew Mole.

Plate X

Drawn on Stone by W.E.Hitchcock.

Lith⁴ Printed & Col⁴ by J.T Bowen, Philad⁴

Drawn from Nature by J.J.Audubon.F.R.S.F.L.S

Common American Shrew Mole.

Male & Female

Plate CXLV

N°.29

Drawn from Nature by J.W. Audubon

On Stone by Wᵐ E. Hitchcock

Lith Printed & Col.ᵈ by J.T.Bowen, Phil

Townsend's Shrew Mole

Black Squirrel.

Drawn from Nature by J.J.Audubon, F.R.S.F.L.S.   Lith.ᵈ Printed & Col.ᵈ by J.T. Bowen, Philadᵃ.

Drawn on Stone by R. Trembly.

Carolina Grey Squirrel.
Male & Female.

Drawn from Nature by J. J. Audubon F.R.S.F.L.S.

Printed by Nagel & Weingærtner, N.Y.

Cat Squirrel

Drawn from Nature by J.J.Audubon FRS FLS   Printed by Nagel & Weingærtner NY

Drawn on Stone by R.Trembly   Colored by J.Lawrence

Plate CLIII

Fig 1

Fig 2

Fig 1 *Col. Albert's Squirrel.* — Fig 2. *California Grey Squirrel.*

Drawn from Nature by J.W. Audubon

Lith Printed & Col.ᵈ by J.T. Bowen, Phil

Plate CIV

On Stone by Wm E. Hitchcock

Collies Squirrel

Drawn from Nature by J. W. Audubon.

Lith. Printed & Col.ª by J. T. Bowen, Ph.

Drawn on Stone by J. T. Trembly

Downy Squirrel.

Drawn from Nature by J.J.Audubon F.R.S F.L.S.   Printed by Nagel & Weingærtner N.Y.

On Stone by W.ᵐ H. Hitchcock

Douglass Squirrel.

Drawn from Nature by J.J.Audubon. F.R.S.F.L.S.   Lith Printed & Col.ᵈ by J.T.Bowen, Phil.ᵃ

On Stone by W.E.Hitchcock.

Dusky Squirrel.

Drawn from Nature by J.W.Audubon.   Lith.ᵈ Printed & Col.ᵈ by J.T.Bowen, Philad.ᵃ

Fig 1

Fig 2

On Stone by Wm E. Hitchcock

Fig. 1 Fremont's Squirrel. Fig 2 Sooty Squirrel.

Drawn from Nature by J W Audubon

Lith Printed & Col^d by J T Bowen, Phil.

Fox Squirrel.

Drawn from Nature by J.J.Audubon. F.R.S.F.L.S.

Lith. Printed & Col.d by J.T. Bowen, Phil.

Drawn on Stone by W.E. Hitchcock.

Hare Squirrel.

Hudson's Bay Squirrel - Chickaree - Red Squirrel.

Drawn from Nature by J.J. Audubon F.R.S.,F.L.S.

Drawn on Stone by R. Trembly.

Printed by Nagel & Weingærtner N.Y.

Colored by J. Lawrence

Drawn on stone by R. Trembly

Long Haired Squirrel.

Drawn from Nature by J.J.Audubon, FRS.FLS.

Printed & Col.d by J.T. Bowen, Philad

Stone by Wᵐ E. Hitchcock

Migratory Squirrel.

Drawn from Nature by J.J.Audubon,F.R.S.F.L.S.

Lith. Printed & Colᵈ by J.T.Bowen, Phil.

Plate LVIII.

On Stone by W.E. Hitchcock

Orange-bellied Squirrel.

Drawn from Nature by J.J. Audubon, P.R.S.F.L.S.   Lith.ᵈ Printed & Col.ᵈ by J.T. Bowen, Philad.ᵃ

Red-Bellied Squirrel.

Drawn from Nature by J.J. Audubon, F.R.S. F.L.S.

Lithᵈ Printed & Colᵈ by J.T. Bowen, Philadᵃ

On Stone by W.F. Hitchcock

Red-tailed Squirrel.

Drawn from Nature by J.J. Audubon, F.R.S.F.L.S   Lith. Printed & Col.d by J.T. Bowen, Philada

Plate V

Drawn on Stone by Wᵐ E. Hitchcock

Richardson's Columbian Squirrel

Drawn from Nature by J.J. Audubon, F.R.S.F.L.S.

Lith. Printed & Colᵈ by J.T.Bowen, Phil

Plate LXXXIX

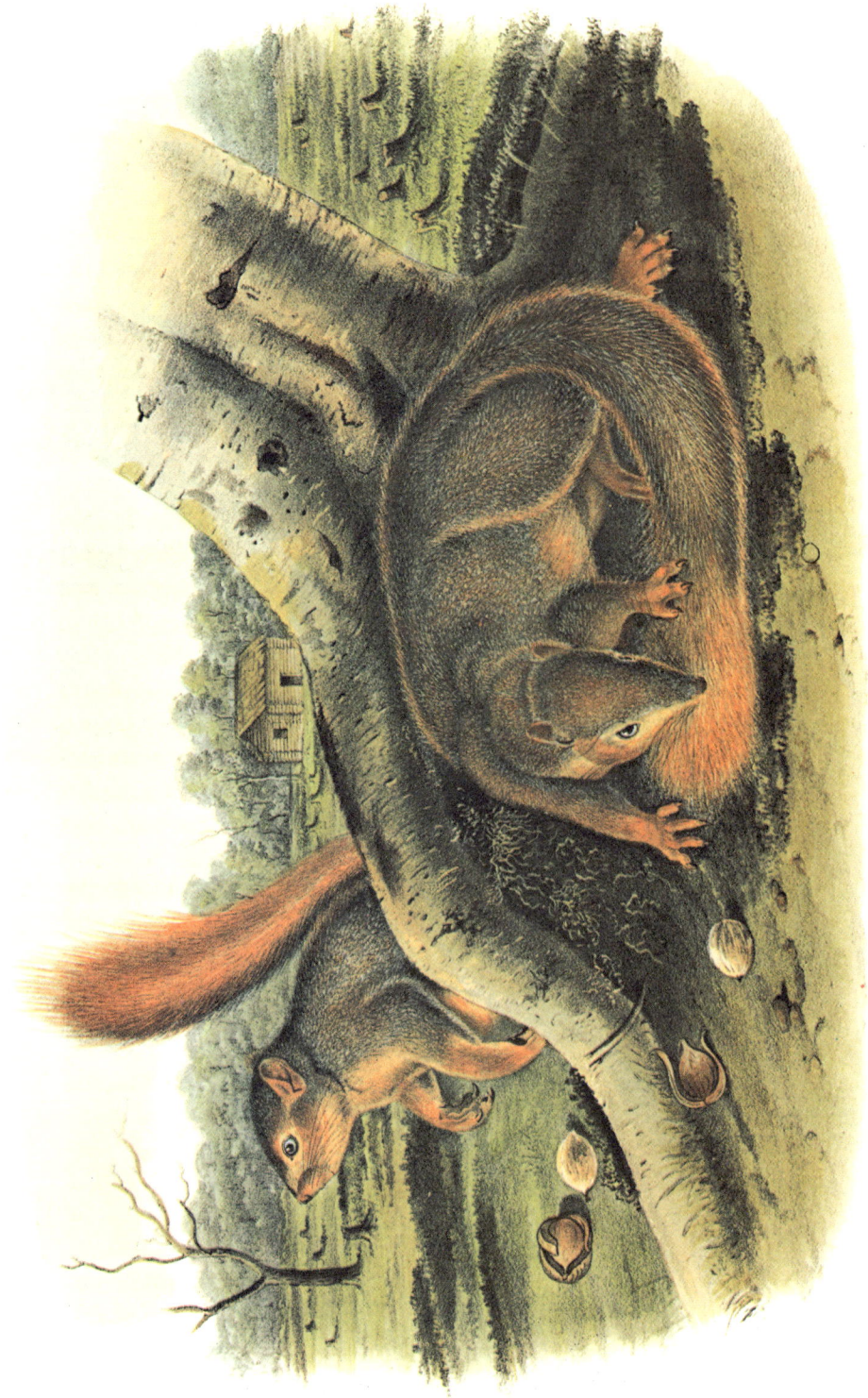

On Stone by Wᵐ E Hitchcock

Lith. Printed & Colᵈ by J T Bowen, Philad

Say's Squirrel

Drawn from Nature by J.J.Audubon, F.R.S.F.L.S.

628

Plate XIX

Soft haired Squirrel.

Drawn from Nature by J.J.Audubon F.R.S.F.L.S.

Printed by Nagel & Weingærtner, N.Y.

Drawn on Stone by R.Trembly.

Drawn on Stone by W.ᵐ E. Hitchcock.

Fig.1 *Weasel - like Squirrel*

Fig.2 *Large Louisiana Black Squirrel.*

Drawn from Nature by J.W. Audubon.   Lith. Printed & Col.ᵈ by J.T. Bowen, Phil.

Plate XXX

N.° 6

Drawn on Stone by R. Trembly.

Cotton Rat.

Printed by Nagel & Weingærtner NY

Drawn from Nature by J.J. Audubon. F.R.S, F.L.S.

Plate CXXV

N° 25

Drawn from Nature by J.W.Audubon.

Lith. Printed & Col.d by J.T. Bowen Phil.

American Marsh Shrew

Plate LXXV.

On Stone by Wᵐ E. Hitchcock

Lith. Printed & Colᵈ by J T. Bowen. Phil.

Drawn from Nature by J. J. Audubon, F R S F L S

Carolina Shrew

633

Plate LXX.

On Stone by Wm E. Hitchcock

Lith. Printed & Col^d by J. T. Bowen, Philad

Say's Least Shrew.

Drawn from Nature by J. J. Audubon, F.R.S.F.L.S.

634

Plate LXXIX

On Stone by Wᵐ E. Hitchcock.

Drawn from Nature by J. Audubon, F.R.S.F.L.S

Lith. Printed & Col.ᵈ by J. T. Bowen, Phil.

Annulated Marmot Squirrel.

Plate XLIX

Drawn from Nature by J. J. Audubon FRS FLS

Douglasses Spermophile

Lith.d Printed & Col.d by J. T. Bowen Philad.a

On stone by W.E. Hitchcock

Lith.ᵈ Printed & Col.ᵈ by J.T.Bowen Philad.ᵃ

Franklin's Marmot Squirrel.

Drawn from Nature by J.J.Audubon F.R.S.FL.S.

Plate CLIV

Fig 1

Fig 2

Drawn from Nature by J.W.Audubon.

On Stone by Wm F. Hitchcock

Lith. Printed & Col.d by J.T. Bowen, Phil

Fig 1 Harris' Marmot Squirrel   Fig 2 California Meadow Mouse

Drawn from Nature by J.J.Audubon. F.R.S. F.L.S.

Drawn on Stone by R.Trembly

Lith. Printed & Col.ᵈ by J.T.Bowen, Ph.ᵃ

Leopard, Spermophile.

Large-tailed Spermophile

No 28

640

Plate. CIX

N.º 22.

Drawn on Stone by Wᵐ E. Hitchcock

Drawn from Nature by J.W.Audubon

Mexican Marmot-Squirrel.

Adult male and young.

Lith. Printed & Colᵈ by J.T.Bowen, Phil

Plate IX

Drawn from Nature by J.J.Audubon, F.R.S.F.L.S.

On Stone by Wᵐ E. Hitchcock

Lith. Printed & Colᵈ by J.T. Bowen, Phil

Parry's Marmot Squirrel

Plate XCIX.

N° 20

On Stone by W^m. E. Hitchcock

Lith. Printed & Col^d by J.T. Bowen, Phil^a

Drawn from Nature by J.J.Audubon, F.R.S.F.L.S.

Prairie Dog. — Prairie Marmot Squirrel.

Plate L.

Drawn from Nature by J.J.Audubon, F.R.S.F.L.S.

Richardson's Spermophile

Lith.? Printed & Col.d by J.T.Bowen, Philad.a

Plate CXIV.

Drawn on stone by W.E. Hitchcock

Lith. Printed & Col.d by J.T. Bowen, Philad.a

Say's Marmott Squirrel.

Drawn from Nature by J.W. Audubon

Drawn on Stone by R. Trembly

Chipping Squirrel, Hackee.

Drawn from Nature by J.J.Audubon F.R.S, F.L.S.   Printed by Nagel & Weingaertner N.Y

Plate XXIV

Drawn on Stone by R. Trembly

Printed by Nagel & Weingærtner NY.

Four-striped Ground Squirrel.
1. Male, 2. Female, 3 & 4. Young.

Drawn from Nature by J. J. Audubon F.R.S., F.L.S.

Plate XX

Nº 4

Townsend's Ground Squirrel

Drawn from Nature by J J Audubon F R S F L S

Drawn on Stone by R Trembly

Printed by Nagel & Weingärtner N.Y.

Colored by J Lawrence

648

Plate CXLI

Nº 29.

Drawn from Nature by J. W. Audubon

On Stone by W. E. Hitchcock

American Black Bear

Lith. Printed & Col'd by J.T. Bowen Phil'a

Plate CXXVII.

N°.26.

On stone by W.E. Hitchcock

Lith⁴ Printed & Col⁴ by J.T. Bowen, Philad⁴

Cinnamon Bear.

Drawn from Nature by J.W. Audubon.

650

Plate CXXXI.

On stone by W.E.Hitchcock

Grizzly Bear.

Lith Printed & Col.d by J.T Bowen, Philad.

Drawn from Nature by J.W.Audubon.

Plate XCI

On Stone by Wm E. Hitchcock

Polar Bear.

652

Plate CXVI.

N.º 24.

On Stone by W.E.Hitchcock.

Lith.d Printed & Col.d by J.T.Bowen, Philad.ª

American Black or Silver Fox.

Drawn from Nature by J.W.Audubon.

Plate V

Drawn from Nature by J.J. Audubon F.R.S. F.L.S.
Drawn on Stone by R. Trembly

American Cross Fox.

Printed by Nagel & Weingærtner N.Y

Plate LXXXVII.

Drawn from Nature by J.J. Audubon, FRSFLS   On Stone by Wm E Hitchcock   Lith Printed & Cold by J.T. Bowen, Philad

American Red-Fox.

Plate CXXI

N° 25

Drawn on Stone by Wm E.Hitchcock

Arctic Fox.

Drawn from Nature by J.W.Audubon.

Lith. Printed & Col.d by J T Bowen Phil

Plate XXI

Gray Fox.
Male.

Drawn from Nature by J.J.Audubon F.R.S. F.L.S.

Printed by Nagel & Weingærtner N.Y.

Plate CLI

On Stone by Wᵐ E Hitchcock

Lith. Printed & Col.ᵈ by J.T.Bowen, Phil

Jackall Fox.

Drawn from Nature by J.W. Audubon

Plate LII.

Drawn from Nature by J.J Audubon, F.R.S. F.L.S.

Drawn on Stone by Wm E. Hitchcock.

Swift Fox.

Lith. Printed & Col.d by J.T Bowen, Phil.ada

Index

Woodpecker, Ivory-Billed	*Picus principalis*	280
Woodpecker, Lewis'	*Picus torquatus*	281
Woodpecker, Maria's	*Picus Martinæ*	282
Woodpecker, Missouri Red-Moustached	*Picus Ayresii*	283
Woodpecker, Phillip's	*Picus Phillipsii*	284
Woodpecker, Pileated	*Picus pileatus*	285
Woodpecker, Red-Bellied	*Picus carolinus*	286
Woodpecker, Red-Breasted	*Picus ruber*	287
Woodpecker, Red-Cockaded	*Picus querulus*	288
Woodpecker, Red-Headed	*Picus erythrocephalus*	289
Woodpecker, Red-Shafted	*Picus Mexicanus*	290
Woodpecker, Yellow-Bellied	*Picus varius*	291
Wood-Wagtail *see* Wagtail		
Wood-Warbler, Audubon's	*Sylvicola Audubonii*	81
Wood-Warbler, Bay-Breasted	*Sylvicola castanea*	82
Wood-Warbler, Black-and-Yellow	*Sylvicola maculosa*	83
Wood-Warbler, Blackburnian	*Sylvicola Blackburniæ*	84
Wood-Warbler, Black-Poll	*Sylvicola striata*	85
Wood-Warbler, Black-Throated Blue	*Sylvicola Canadensis*	86
Wood-Warbler, Black-Throated Grey	*Silvicola nigrescens*	88
Wood-Warbler, Blue Yellow-Backed	*Sylvicola Americana*	90
Wood-Warbler, Cape May	*Sylvicola maritima*	91
Wood-Warbler, Cerulian	*Sylvicola coerulea*	93
Wood-Warbler, Chestnut-Sided	*Sylvicola icterocephala*	92
Wood-Warbler, Connecticut	*Sylvicola agilis*	94
Wood-Warbler, Hemlock	*Sylvicola parus*	95
Wood-Warbler, Hermit	*Sylvicola Occidentalis*	96
Wood-Warbler, Pine-Creeping	*Sylvicola pinus*	97
Wood-Warbler, Prairie	*Sylvicola discolor*	98
Wood-Warbler, Rathbone's	*Sylvicola Rathbonii*	99
Wood-Warbler, Townsend's	*Sylvicola Townsendi*	100
Wood-Warbler, Yellow-Crowned	*Sylvicola coronata*	101
Wood-Warbler, Yellow-Poll	*Sylvicola æstiva*	102
Wood-Warbler, Yellow Red-Poll	*Sylvicola petechia*	103
Wood-Warbler, Yellow-Throated	*Sylvicola pensilis*	104
Wood-Warblers *see* Warblers		
Wren, Bewick's	*Troglodytes Bewickii*	121
Wren, Great Carolina	*Troglodytes ludovicianus*	122
Wren, House	*Troglodytes aedon*	124
Wren, Marsh	*Troglodytes palustris*	123
Wren, Parkman's	*Troglodytes Parkmanii*	125
Wren, Rock	*Troglodytes obsoletus*	126
Wren, Short-Billed Marsh	*Troglodytes brevirostris*	127
Wren, Winter	*Troglodytes hyemalis*	128
Wren, Wood	*Troglodytes Americanus*	129
Yellow-Throat, Maryland	*Trichas Marilandica*	107

BIRDS—LATIN–ENGLISH

Agelaius gubernator	Red-and-Black-Shouldered Marsh Blackbird	225
Agelaius phoeniceus	Red-Winged Starling	227
Agelaius tricolor	Red-and-White-Winged Troopial	226
Agelaius xanthocephalus	Yellow-Headed Troopial	228
Alauda alpestris	Shore Lark	156
Alauda rufa	Western Shore Lark	158
Alauda Spragueii	Sprague's Missouri Lark	157
Alca impennis	Great Auk	484
Alca torda	Razor-Billed Auk	485
Alcedo alcyon	Belted Kingfisher	271
Ammodramus caudacutus	Sharp-Tailed Finch	185
Ammodramus Macgillivrayi	MacGillivray's Shore Finch	183
Ammodramus maritimus	Sea-Side Finch	184
Ammodramus palustris	Swamp Sparrow	186
Anas acuta	Pintail Duck	410
Anas Americana	American Widgeon	403
Anas boschas	Mallard Duck	409
Anas Breweri	Brewer's Duck	406
Anas carolinensis	American Green-Winged Teal	404
Anas clypeata	Shoveller Duck	411
Anas discors	Blue-Winged Teal	405
Anas obscura	Dusky Duck	407
Anas sponsa	Wood Duck	412
Anas strepera	Gadwall Duck	408
Anser albifrons	White-Fronted Goose	397
Anser bernicla	Brent Goose	395
Anser Canadensis	Canada Goose	396
Anser Hutchinsii	Hutchins's Goose	398
Anser hyperboreus	Snow Goose	399
Anser leucopsis	Bernacle Goose	394
Anthus ludovicianus	Titlark	155
Aphriza Townsendi	Townsend's Surf-Bird	340
Aquila chrysaëtos	Golden Eagle	14
Aramus scolopaceus	Scolopaceous Courlan	330
Ardea candidissima	Snowy Heron	391
Ardea coerulea	Blue Heron	383
Ardea egretta	Great American White Egret	384
Ardea exilis	Least Bittern	388
Ardea herodias	Great Blue Heron	385
Ardea lentiginosa	American Bittern	381
Ardea Ludoviciana	Louisiana Heron	389

666

669